I0150708

THE

Catholic Devotional

FOR

Confederate Soldiers

"And the smoke of the incenses of the prayers of the saints ascended from the hand of the Angel before God." — Apoc. 8:4

PUBLISHED WITH THE APPROBATION OF

Rt. Rev. J. McGill

BISHOP OF RICHMOND

Edited by

Dr. William G. Peters

CHATTANOOGA:

C. S. Printing Office

2014

Published by the CONFEDERATE STATES PRINTING OFFICE[1], CONFEDERATE STATES OF AMERICA, INC.[2]

---

[1] A division of the CONFEDERATE STATES OF AMERICA, INC.
[2] Also designated the C.S. PRINTING OFFICE

CONTENTS

FOREWORD

This work by Bishop John McGill, Confederate Bishop of Richmond, Virginia, is the second publication in what it is hoped will be many more, by Confederate authors on various subjects of interest to Confederate Americans and others.

Ordained to the priesthood in 1835, in 1850 John McGill became the third bishop of Richmond, being appointed by Blessed Pope Pius IX. He was consecrated on 10 November 1851 from Arbp. Peter Kenrick, with Bishops Richard Miles, O.P., and Martin Spalding serving as co-consecrators.

Bishop McGill was the author of two other works, including *The True Church Indicated to the Inquirer,* and *Faith, The Victory,* originally republished following Lincoln's War as *The Creed of Catholics.* Bishop McGill died at Richmond, 14 January, 1872.

His work, *The True Church*, has already been published by the C.S. PRINTING OFFICE. and *Faith, The Victory* will hopefully soon be reprinted, also by the CONFEDERATE STATES PRINTING OFFICE.

As Bishop McGill states in the Preface, he had *The Angel of Prayer* published for the benefit of Confederate Soldiers so that they might have access to Catholic devotions. Consequently we have renamed this edition, *The Catholic Devotional for Confederate Soldiers*.

Scriptures are from the REAL Douay Rheims, the official Bible of the Catholic Church, and not the Challoner[3] translation used by Bp. McGill.[4]

In the struggle for survival of Christian religion and Confederate culture, we must not forget that while we must work as if everything depends upon us, we must pray for everything depends on God's grace and blessing.

Prayer and devotions were much a part of the Confederate Army, for it considered itself above all, a *Christian* Army.

In this regard, I recommend a prayer for family and daily devotions for our Confederate States first given by President Jefferson Davis.

A PRAYER FOR THE CONFEDERATE STATES

Almighty God, the Sovereign disposer of events, it hath pleased thee to protect and defend the CONFEDERATE STATES, hitherto in their conflict with their enemies, and be unto them a shield.

With grateful thanks we recognize thy hand, and acknowledge that not unto us, but unto Thee belongeth the victory, and in humble dependence upon thy Almighty strength, and trusting in the justness of our cause. We appeal to Thee, that it may please Thee to set at naught the efforts of all our enemies, and put them to confusion and shame.

---

[3] Bp. Challoner's translation of the Bible is commonly sold as the Douay Rheims, but it is not. Cardinal Wiseman has said, "To call it any longer the Doway or Rhemish version is an abuse of terms. It has been altered and modified till scarce any verse remains as it was originally published." http://www.bible-researcher.com/challoner.html

[4] The Orignal and True Douay Rheims©, (also referred to as the REAL Douay Rheims©) copyrighted 2004, 2005 by Dr. William G. von Peters, Ph.D. See www.realdouayrheims.com

O, Almighty God! we pray Thee, that it may please Thee, to grant us Thy blessing upon our arms, and give us victory over all our enemies wherever they may be; preserve our homes and Altars from pollution, and secure to us the restoration of peace and prosperity — all of which we ask in the name of JESUS CHRIST, our blessed Lord and Saviour—to whom with the Father and the Holy Spirit, we will give all the praise and glory in time and throughout all eternity! Amen.

DEO VINDICE!

Dr. William G. Peters
President
THE CONFEDERATE STATES OF AMERICA, INC.
Anno Domini 2014

PREFACE

———————

The difficulty of obtaining books of devotion, under the circumstances resulting from the war, and the necessity of meeting the frequent demands that are made by our Catholic soldiers and citizens for a cheap and portable prayer–book, is our excuse for presenting to the public the present little compilation.

It may not contain all that some may desire to find in it, but, as an aid for the most essential practices of Christian life, we are confident that it will be kindly welcomed, and especially by those who are not already supplied with some other manual of piety.

Bishop John McGill
Richmond, Nov. 1861

A TABLE OF MOVEABLE FEASTS

Year of our Lord	D. Letter	Ash Wednesday	Easter Sunday	Whit Sunday	Corpus Christi	1st Sunday in Advent
1861	F	13 Feb.	31 Mar.	19 May	30 May	1 Dec.
1862	E	5 Mar.	20 Apr.	8 June	10 June	30 Nov.
1863	P	18 Feb.	20 Apr.	8 June	19 June	20 Nov.
1864	CB	10 Feb.	27 Mar.	15 May	26 May	27 Nov.
1865	A	1 Mar.	16 Apr.	4 June	15 June	3 Dec.
1866	G	14 Feb.	1 Apr.	20 May	31 May	2 Dec.
1867	F	6 Mar.	21 Apr.	9 June	20 June	1 Dec.
1868	ED	26 Feb.	12 Mar.	31 May	11 June	29 Nov.
1869	C	10 Feb.	28 Mar.	16 May	27 May	28 Nov.
1870	B	2 Mar.	17 Apr.	5 June	16 June	27 Nov.
1871	A	22 Feb.	9 Apr.	28 May	8 June	3 Dec.
1872	GF	13 Feb.	31 Mar.	19 May	30 May	1 Dec.
1873	E	26 Feb.	1 Apr.	1 June	12 June	30 Nov.
1874	D	18 Feb.	5 Apr.	24 May	4 June	29 Nov.

The manner of lay persons' baptizing an infant in danger of death.

Take common water, and pour it on the head or face of the child, and while you are pouring it, say the following words:

"I baptize thee in the name of the Father, and of the Son, and of the Holy Ghost. *Amen.*"

NOTE.—Any person, whether man, woman or child, may baptize an infant, in case of danger of death.

SHORT PRAYERS DURING THE DAY

Before Meals.

Bless us, O Lord! and these thy gifts, which we are about to receive from thy bounty: through Christ our Lord. Amen.

After Meals.

We give thee thanks, O Almighty God! for all thy benefits, who livest and reignest, world without end. Amen.

Before Work, or Study.

To thee O Lord! I offer the work, which, in compliance with thy holy will, I am about to begin; give it thy blessing, that it may contribute to thy glory, and my salvation.

Invocation of the Holy Ghost.

V. Come, O Holy Spirit! fill the hearts of thy Faithful.

R. And kindle in them the fire of thy divine love.

Let us pray.

O God! who, by the light of the Holy Ghost, didst instruct the hearts of the Faithful, give us by the same Holy Spirit, a love and relish of what is right and just, and a constant enjoyment of his comforts: through Christ our Lord. Amen.

𝔉𝔢𝔞𝔰𝔱𝔰 𝔄𝔫𝔡 𝔉𝔞𝔰𝔱𝔰

THROUGHOUT THE YEAR

Holy days on which there is a strict obligation to hear Mass, and refrain from servile works.

All Sundays in the year.

The Feast of the Circumcision of our Lord, Jan: 1.

The Epiphany, Jan. 6.

The Annunciation, March 25.

Ascension of our Lord.

Corpus Christi.

Assumption of the B. V. Mary, August 15.

Feast of All Saints, November 1

Nativity of our Lord, Dec. 25

Fasting Days

All days in Lent, except Sundays. The Eve of Whitsuntide.

The Quarter-Tenses, or Ember days, that occur in the four seasons of the year.

The Vigil of the Assumption of the Blessed Virgin Mary, and of All Saints.

Every Friday in Advent, and Christmas Eve.

Days of Abstinence from Flesh Meat.

Every Day in Lent except when the use of meat is allowed by the Archbishop or Bishop of the diocese.

All Fridays in the year.

If a fasting day fall on a Sunday, the fast is kept on the Saturday before. If Christmas Day fall upon a Friday, neither fast nor abstinence is observed.

N. B.—The Catholic Church commands all her children to be present at the great Eucharistic Sacrifice, which we call the Mass; and to rest from servile work on Sundays and Holydays.

Fasting Days

Secondly, To abstain from flesh on all the days of fasting and abstinence.

Thirdly, To confess their sins at least once a year.

Fourthly, To receive the blessed sacrament at least once a year, during Easter time.

The time for satisfying the Easter precept in the States, as well North as South, is, in virtue of a late concession, from the first Sunday of Lent to Trinity Sunday, both inclusively.

Before prayer prepare thy soul: and be not as a man that tempteth God. — Eccles. 18:23.

But in every thing, by prayer and supplication, with thanksgiving, let your petitions be known to God. — Phil. 4:6

But thou when thou shalt pray, enter into thy chamber, and having shut the door, pray to thy father in secret: and thy father which seeth in secret, will repay thee. — Matt. 6:6

And all things whatsoever you shall ask in prayer believing, you shall receive. — Matt. 21:22

Attend to the voice of my prayer, my King and my God. Because I will pray to Thee: Lord, in the morning Thou wilt hear my voice. — Ps. 5:3-4

The Angelus Domini

To be said Morning, Noon, and Night, in Memory of our Saviour's becoming Man for our Salvation.

1. The angel of the Lord declared unto Mary; and she conceived of the Holy Ghost. Hail, Mary, &c. 2. Behold the handmaid of the Lord. May it be done unto me according to thy word. Hail, Mary, &c. 3. And the Word was made flesh; and dwelt among us. Hail, Mary, &c.

Let us Pray.

POUR forth, we beseech Thee, O Lord, thy grace into our hearts, that we, to whom the incarnation of Christ, thy Son, was made known by the message of an angel, may by his passion and cross be brought to the glory of his resurrection: through the same Christ our Lord. Amen.

The Regina Coeli[5]

O Queen of Heaven! rejoice, Alleluia;

For he whom thou didst deserve to bear, Alleluia,

Is risen again, as he said. Alleluia. Pray for us to God. Alleluia.

V. Rejoice and be glad, O Virgin Mary! Alleluia.

R. Because our Lord is truly risen. Alleluia.

Let us Pray.

O God! who by the Resurrection of thy Son, our Lord Jesus Christ, hast been pleased to fill the world with gladness,

---

[5] To be said instead of the Angelus, from Holy Saturday, at noon, till noon before Trinity Sunday.

grant, we beseech thee, that by the intercession of the Virgin Mary, his mother, we may obtain the joys of eternal life: through the same Christ our Lord. R. Amen.

𝔐orning 𝔈xercises

[Awaking in the morning, say:]

O my God! my only good! the author of my being and my last end! I give thee my heart. Praise, honor, and glory be to thee for ever and ever. Amen.

[Rising, say:]

In the name of the Father, and of the Son, and of the Holy Ghost. Amen.

I will raise myself up from this bed of sleep, to adore my God: and to labor for the salvation of my soul. Oh! may I rise on the last day, unto life everlasting!

[When clothed, kneel down, and say:]

In the name of the Father, and of the Son, and of the Holy Ghost. *Amen.*

BLESSED be the holy and undivided Trinity now, and for ever more. Holy, Holy, Holy, Lord God of hosts! The earth is full of thy Glory. Glory be to the Father! Glory' be to the Son! Glory be to the Holy Ghost!

ACT OF ADORATION

O GREAT God! the sovereign Lord of heaven and earth! I prostrate myself before thee. With all the angels and saints I adore thee. I acknowledge thee to be my Creator and sovereign Lord, my first beginning, and last end. I render to thee the homage of my being and life. I submit myself to thy holy will, and I devote myself to thy divine service this day and for ever.

AN ACT OF FAITH

O MY God! I firmly believe all the sacred truths, which thy holy Catholic Church believes and teaches; because thou hast revealed them, who canst neither deceive, nor be deceived.

AN ACT OF HOPE

O my God! relying on thy infinite goodness and promises, I hope to obtain the pardon of my sins, the assistance of thy grace, and life everlasting; through the merits of Jesus Christ, my Lord, and Redeemer.

AN ACT OF LOVE

O my God! I love thee above all things with my whole heart and soul, because thou art infinitely amiable, and deserving of all love. I love also my neighbor as myself for the love of thee. I forgive all who have injured me, and ask pardon of all, whom I have injured.

AN ACT OF THANKSGIVING

O GLORIOUS Trinity! I praise thee and give thee thanks for the numberless benefits thou host bestowed upon me. I thank thee, O heavenly Father! for having created me to thy own image and likeness, and for having preserved me to this day. I thank thee, O merciful Son for having redeemed me by thy death. and so often fed me with thy precious body and blood. I thank thee, O holy Spirit! for having cleansed my soul by thy grace in holy baptism, for having called me to the true faith, and so often washed me from my sins in the sacrament of penance. I thank thee, O most bountiful God for having preserved me this night, and for granting me this day to serve thee. I earnestly invite all the saints of heaven and earth, to join with me in praise and thanksgiving for thy infinite goodness.

[Pause a while, and foresee the sins you are most subject to; and firmly resolve to avoid them.]

AN ACT OF CONTRITION

O MY God! I am most heartily sorry for all my sins, and I detest them above all things from the bottom of my heart, because they displease thee, my God, who art most deserving of all my love for thy most amiable and adorable perfections; and I firmly propose, by thy holy grace, never more to offend thee, and to do all that I can to atone for my sins.

A RESOLUTION TO AVOID EVIL AND TO DO GOOD

ADORABLE Jesus! Divine Model of that perfection to which we should all aspire! I will endeavor, this day, to follow thy example; to be mild, humble, chaste, zealous, patient, charitable and resigned. Incline my heart to keep thy commandments. I am resolved to watch over myself with the greatest diligence, and to live soberly, justly and piously, for the time to come. I will take care of tiny ways, that I may not offend with my tongue. I will turn away my eyes, that they may not see vanity; and I will be particularly attentive not to relapse r this day, into my accustomed failings, but to struggle against them with thy gracious assistance. Enlighten my mind, purify my heart, and guide my steps, that I may pass all, my life in thy divine service. *Amen.*

OFFER YOURSELF WITHOUT RESERVE TO GOD

O LORD! I offer thee my whole being, and particularly all my thoughts, words, and actions of this day, together with all the crosses and contradictions, I may meet with, in the course of it. I consecrate them entirely to the glory of thy name, in union with those of Jesus Christ, my Saviour, that through his infinite merits, they may all find acceptance. Give them, O Lord! a blessing. May thy divine love animate them; and may they all tend to the greater honor of thy sovereign Majesty. *Amen.*

IMPLORE THE NECESSARY GRACES

THOU knowest, O God! my weakness; that I am poor and destitute; that I cannot do, that I cannot even think of any good without thee. Rise up, then, to help me; strengthen me with thy grace, that I may fervently execute what I have firmly resolved, and not only avoid all the evil thou forbiddest, but also perform all the good thou commandest.

THE LORD'S PRAYER

OUR Father, who art in heaven! hallowed be thy name; thy kingdom come; thy will be done on earth, as it is in heaven. Give us this day our daily bread; and forgive us our trespasses, as we forgive them, who trespass against us. And lead us not into temptation; but deliver us from evil. *Amen.*

THE ANGELICAL SALUTATION

HAIL Mary, full of grace! the Lord is with thee; blessed art thou amongst women, and blessed is the fruit of thy womb, Jesus. HOLY Mary, mother of God! pray for us sinners, now, and at the hour of our death. *Amen.*

THE APOSTLES CREED

I BELIEVE in God, the Father Almighty, Creator of heaven and earth, and in Jesus Christ, his only Son, our Lord; 'who was conceived by, the Holy Ghost, born of the Virgin Mary, suffered under Pontius Pilate, was crucified, dead and buried; he descended into hell, the third day he rose again from the dead; he ascended into heaven, and sitteth at the right hand of God the Father Almighty; from thence he shall come to judge the living, and the dead. I believe in the Holy Ghost; the holy Catholic Church; the communion of Saints; the forgiveness of sins; the resurrection of the body, and life everlasting. *Amen.*

THE CONFITEOR

I CONFESS to Almighty God, to blessed Mary ever Virgin, to blessed Michael the Archangel, to blessed John the Baptist, to the holy apostles Peter and Paul, and to all the saints, that I have sinned exceedingly in thought, word, and deed, through my fault, through my fault, through my most grievous fault. Therefore I beseech the blessed Mary ever Virgin, the blessed Michael the Archangel, the blessed John the Baptist, the holy Apostles Peter and Paul, and all the saints, to pray to the Lord our God, for me.

May the Almighty God have mercy on me, forgive me my sins, and bring me to everlasting life! *Amen.*

May the Almighty and merciful Lord give me pardon, absolution, and remission of all my sins! *Amen.*

Invoke the blessed Virgin, your angel guardian,
and your patron saint.

O HOLY Virgin, Mother of God! my advocate and patroness I pray for thy poor servant, show thyself a mother to me. And thou, O blessed Spirit, whom God in his mercy hath appointed to watch over me, intercede for me this day, that I may not stray from the path of virtue. Thou also, O happy saint! whose name I bear, pray for me, that I may serve God faithfully in this life, as thou hast done, and glorify him eternally with thee in heaven. *Amen.*

LITANY OF THE HOLY NAME OF JESUS

Lord, have mercy on us. Christ have mercy on us. Lord, have mercy on us.
Christ, hear us.
Christ, graciously hear us.

God, the Father of heaven, *Have mercy on us.*
God, the Son, Redeemer of the world,
God, the Holy Ghost,

Holy Trinity, one God,
Jesus, son of the living God,
Jesus, splendor of the Father,
Jesus, brightness of eternal light,
Jesus, king of glory,
Jesus, sun of justice,
Jesus, son of the Virgin Mary,
Jesus, most amiable,
Jesus, most admirable,
Jesus, powerful God,
Jesus, father of the world to come,
Jesus, angel of the great council,
Jesus, most patient,
Jesus, most obedient,
Jesus, meek and humble of heart,
Jesus, lover of chastity,
Jesus, God of peace,
Jesus, lover of mankind,
Jesus, author of life,
Jesus, model of virtues,
Jesus, zealous for souls,
Jesus, our God,
Jesus, our refuge,
Jesus, father of the poor,
Jesus, treasure, of the faithful,
Jesus, good shepherd,
Jesus, true light,
Jesus, eternal wisdom,
Jesus, infinite goodness,
Jesus, our way and our life,
Jesus, joy of angels,
Jesus, king of the patriarchs,
Jesus, master of the apostles,
Jesus, teacher of the evangelists,
Jesus, strength of martyrs;
Jesus, light of confessors,
Jesus, purity of virgins!
Jesus, crown of all saints!
Be merciful unto us. *Hear us, O Jesus!*

Be merciful unto us. *Spare us, O Jesus!*
From all evil, *Lord Jesus Deliver us!*
From all sin,
From thy wrath,
From the snares of the devil,
From the spirit of uncleanness,
From eternal death;
From the neglect of thy inspirations,
Through the mystery of thy incarnation,
Through thy childhood,
Through thy most sacred life,
Through thy labors,
Through thy agony and passion,
Through thy death and burial,
Through thy resurrection,
Through thy ascension,
Through thy joys,
Through thy nativity,
Through thy glory.
Lamb of God who takest away the sins of the world! *Spare us, O Jesus!*
Lamb of God! who takest away the sins of the world! *Hear us, O Jesus!*
Lamb of God! who takest away the sins of the world! *Have mercy on us, O Jesus!*
Jesus, hear us. *Lord Jesus, graciously hear us.*

Let us pray

O LORD Jesus Christ! Who has said, *ask, and thou shalt receive; seek, and thou shalt find; knock, and it shall be opened unto thee*; mercifully attend to our supplications, and grant us the divine gift of thy charity, that we may ever love thee with our whole hearts, and never desist from thy praise; who livest and reignest one God, world without end. *Amen.*

Evening Exercises

In the name of the Father, and of the Son, and of the Holy Ghost. Amen.

BLESSED be the holy and undivided Trinity, now and for ever. *Amen.*

Come, O Holy Ghost! replenish the hearts of thy faithful, and kindle in them the fire of thy divine love.

ACT OF ADORATION

GREAT God! the Lord of heaven and earth! I prostrate myself before thee. With all the angels and saints, I adore thee. I acknowledge thee to be my Creator and sovereign Lord, my first beginning and last end. I render to thee the homage of my being and life. I submit myself to thy holy will; and I devote myself to thy divine service, now and for ever.

AN ACT OF FAITH

O MY God! I firmly believe all the sacred truths, which thy holy Catholic Church believes and teaches; because thou hast revealed them, who canst neither deceive, nor be deceived.

AN ACT OF HOPE

O MY God! relying on thy infinite goodness and promises, I hope to obtain the pardon of my sins, the assistance of thy grace, and life everlasting, through the merits of Jesus Christ, my Lord, and Redeemer.

AN ACT OF LOVE.

O MY God! I love thee above all things with my whole heart and soul, because thou art infinitely amiable and deserving of all love. I love also my neighbor as myself, for the love of thee. I forgive all who have injured me, and ask pardon of all, whom I have injured.

LET US RETURN THANKS TO GOD FOR THE FAVORS BESTOWED ON US

How shall I be able to thank thee, O Lord! for all thy favors? Thou hast thought of me from all eternity; thou hast brought me forth from nothing; thou hast given thy life to redeem me, and thou continuest still, daily, to load me with thy favors. Alas! my God! what return can I make thee, for all thy benefits, and in particular for the favors of this day! Join me, ye blessed spirits! and all ye elect! in praising the God of mercies, who is so, bountiful to so unworthy a creature.

LET US BEG OF GOD TO MAKE KNOWN OUR SINS TO US

O HOLY Ghost, eternal source of light! remove my darkness, and dispel those shades, that hide from me the filth and enormity of my offences. Show me, I beseech thee, the sins I have this day committed, in thought, word, and action. Grant me a feeling sense of them, that I may detest them all from the bottom of my heart, and dread nothing so much, as ever to commit them hereafter.

Let us examine our consciences, and consider where we have been this day, and in what company. Let us call to mind the duties of our state, and our different offences.

Against God. By omissions, negligence in our religious duties, irreverence in the Church, willful distractions in prayer, faults in our intentions, resistance to divine grace, oaths, murmurings, want of confidence and resignation.

Against our neighbor. By rash judgments, hatred, jealousy, contempt, desire of revenge, quarrelling, passion, imprecations, injuries, detraction, raillery, false reports, damaging either in goods or reputation; bad example, scandal; want of obedience, respect, charity, or fidelity.

Against ourselves. By vanity, human respect, lies; by thoughts, desires, discourse, or actions contrary to purity; by intemperance, rage, impatience; by a useless and sensual life, or sloth in complying with the duties of our state. Recite the general confession, *I confess to Almighty God, &c.*, as in page 11.

A FIRM PURPOSE OF AMENDMENT

O ETERNAL God! against whom I have sinned, I wish from my heart that I had never offended thee; but as I have been so unhappy, O grant me now grace, never more to offend thee. Thou willest not the death of a sinner, but rather that he be converted and live. Convert me then, and I shall be converted. Have mercy on me according to thy great mercy, and according to the multitude of thy tender mercies, blot out my iniquities. I renounce all sin, and firmly purpose to shun all the occasions of it, and to walk henceforth in the path of thy commandments. This is my fixed resolution, which I hope I shall faithfully keep, relying upon thee, through Jesus Christ, our Lord. *Amen.*

LITANY OF THE BLESSED VIRGIN

ANTHEM

WE fly to thy patronage, O holy Mother of God! despise not our petitions in our necessities, but deliver us from all dangers, O ever glorious and blessed Virgin!

Lord, have mercy on us.
Christ, have mercy on us.
Lord, have mercy on us.
Christ, hear us: Christ, graciously hear us.
God the Father of Heaven, *have mercy on us.*
God the Son, Redeemer of the world, *Have mercy on us.*
God the Holy Ghost, *Have mercy on us.*
Holy Trinity, one God, *Have mercy on us.*
Holy Mary, *Pray for us.*
Holy mother of God,
Holy virgin of virgins,
Mother of Christ,
Mother of divine grace,
Mother most pure,
Mother most chaste,
Mother undefiled,
Mother unviolated,
Mother most amiable,
Mother most admirable,
Mother of our Creator,
Mother of our Redeemer,
Virgin most prudent,
Virgin most venerable,
Virgin most renowned,
Virgin most powerful,
Virgin most merciful,
Virgin most faithful,
Mirror of justice,
Seat of wisdom,
Cause of our joy,

Spiritual vessel,
Vessel of honor,
Singular vessel of devotion,
Mystical rose,
Tower of David,
Tower of ivory,
House of gold,
Ark of the covenant,
Gate of heaven,
Morning star,
Health of the sick,
Refuge of sinners,
Comforter of the afflicted,
Help of Christians,
Queen of angels,
Queen of patriarchs,
Queen of prophets,
Queen of apostles,
Queen of martyrs,
Queen of confessors,
Queen of virgins,
Queen of all saints,
Queen conceived without original sin,
Lamb of God, You take away sins of the world, *Spare us, O Lord.*
Lamb of God, You take away the sins of the world, *Graciously hear us, O Lord.*
Lamb of God, Your take away the sins of the world, *Have mercy on us.*
Lord have mercy on us.
V. Pray for us, O holy Mother of God.
R. That we may be made worthy of the promises of Christ.

Let us pray

DEFEND, we beseech thee, O Lord! through the intercession of the blessed Mary, ever virgin, this family from all adversity; and, as in all humility, they prostrate themselves before thee, do thou mercifully protect them against all the snares of their enemies; through Christ, our Lord. *Amen.*

Pour down thy blessing, O Lord! on thy holy Church, on our holy Father the Pope; on this diocese, on our most reverend Archbishop, on our Bishop, and all pastors of souls; on this country, on our rulers, and all superiors, temporal and spiritual; on this congregation; on this family; on our parents, relations, benefactors, friends, and enemies. Help the poor, the sick, and those that are in their agony; convert all heretics, and enlighten the infidels.

Our Father, &c. Hail Mary, &c. I believe in God, &c. See pg. 9.

Let us pray for the souls of all the Faithful departed, particularly for those of our friends and benefactors.

PSALM 129

FROM the depths I have cried to thee, O Lord! Lord hear my voice:

Let thy ears be intent to the voice of my petition.

If thou shalt observe iniquities, O Lord: Lord! who shall stand it.

Because with thee there is propitiation: and for thy law, I have expected thee, O Lord!

My soul hath expected in his word: my soul hath hoped in our Lord.

From the morning watch even until night, let Israel hope in our Lord.

Because with our Lord there is mercy; and with him plenteous redemption.

And he shall redeem Israel, from all his iniquities.

V. Eternal rest give unto them, O Lord!

R. And let perpetual light shine upon them.

May they rest in peace. *Amen.*

V. O Lord! hear my prayer.

R. And let my cry come unto thee.

Let us Pray

O GOD! the Creator and Redeemer of all the faithful, grant to the souls of thy servants departed, the remission of all their sins: that, through pious supplications, they may obtain that pardon, which they have always desired, who livest and reignest world without end. Amen.

Let us recommend our rest to God, to the blessed Virgin, and the Saints

V. Vouchsafe, O Lord! this night, to keep us without sin.
R. Have mercy on us, O Lord! have mercy on us.

Let us Pray

VISIT, we beseech thee, O Lord! this habitation, and drive from it all the snares of the enemy. Let thy holy angels dwell herein, to preserve us in peace; and may thy blessing he upon us for ever, through Jesus Christ our Lord. *Amen.*

Bless, O Lord! the repose I am going to take, in- order to renew my strength, that I may be better able to serve thee. O all ye saints and angels! but chiefly thou. O Mother of God! Intercede for me this night, and during the rest of my life, but particularly at the hour of my death.

May the divine assistance remain always with us. *Amen.*

ANTHEMS

AT

SPRINKLING THE HOLY WATER

BEFORE HIGH MASS.

Before solemn Mass, from Trinity *to* Palm Sunday inclusively, *the following* Anthem is *sung:*

Asperges me, Domine, hyssopo et mundabor,

Lavabis me, et super nivem dealbabor.

Miserere mei, Deus, secundum magnam misericordiam tuam.

V. Gloria, &c.

Ant. Asperges, &c.

Thou wilt sprinkle me, O Lord, with hyssop and I shall be cleansed

Thou wilt wash me, and I shall be washed whiter than snow.

Pity me, O God, according to Thy great mercy.

V. Gloria, &c.

Ant. Sprinkle me, &c.

The Priest being returned to the foot of the Altar, says:

V. Ostende nobis, Domine, misericordiam tuam.

R. Et salutare tuum da nobis.

V. Domine, exaudi orationem meam,

R. Et clamor meus ad te veniat.

V. Dominus vobiscum.

R. Et cum spiritu tuo.

V. Show us, O Lord, Thy mercy,

R. And grant us thy salvation.

V. O Lord, hear my prayer,

R. And let my cry come unto thee.

V. The Lord be with you.

R. And with thy spirit.

For the prayer *Exaudi,* see next page.

From Easter to Whitsunday inclusively, the following is sung:

Vidi aquam egredientem de templo a latere dextro, Alleluia: et omnes ad quos pervenit aqua ista salvi facti sunt, et dicent, Alleluia.

I saw water flowing from the right side of the temple, *Alleluia*: and all to whom that water came were saved, and they shall say, *Alleluia*.

Ps. Confitemini Domino, quoniam bonus: quoniam in saeculum misericordia ejus. Gloria, &c.

Ps. Praise the Lord, for he is good: for his mercy endureth forever. Glory. &c.

The Prayer, *Exaudi.*

Exaudi nos, Domine sancte. Pater Omnipotens, aeterne Deus: et mittere digneris sanctum angelum tuum de coelis, qui custodiat, foveat, protegat, visitet, atque defendat omnes habitantes in hoc habitaculo. Per Christum Dominum nostrum. *Amen.*

Hear us, O holy Lord, almighty Father, everlasting God, and vouchsafe to send Thy holy Angel from heaven, to guard, cherish, protect, visit and defend all that are assembled in this place: through Christ our Lord. *Amen.*

Five Points or Resolutions

Which may be formed with much spiritual profit, either before or after hearing Mass.

I.

I detest and abhor all and every one of the sins I have ever committed, or that have been committed by others from the beginning of the world to the present hour, or that may be hereafter committed to the end thereof; and I would, with the grace of God, do my utmost to prevent them, which I therefore humbly implore.

II

I extol and approve of all the good works that have been done from the beginning of the world, or that may be done hereafter to the consummation thereof: and I would, with the help of God, multiply them, whose grace I most humbly implore.

I purpose henceforth to direct all my thoughts, words and actions, to the greater glory of God, in union with all those good intentions which the saints have ever had—now have—or can possibly have hereafter.

I pardon and forgive, from the bottom of my heart, all my enemies—all who calumniate or detract me, all who would by any means injure me, or wish that evil would befall me.

O! that it were possible I could save all mankind by dying for each individual: this I would freely do by the help of the grace of God, which I therefore earnestly invoke, for without his grace, I can do nothing. — *Ex. Missali Romano.*

Devotions for Mass

A PRAYER BEFORE MASS

O FATHER Of mercies! and God of all consolation! who, not content, that thy only begotten Son should have once been offered a bleeding victim upon the cross for our salvation, wouldst have the same most acceptable oblation, daily repeated in an unbloody manner, to renew in our souls the fruit thereof; grant, we beseech thee, that we may assist at this adorable mystery of thy power, wisdom, and goodness, with such reverence, attention, and love, that we may plentifully partake of the fruits it is intended to produce in us, through the same Jesus Christ, our Lord. Amen

AT THE COMMENCEMENT OF MASS

In the name of the Father, and of the Son, and of the Holy Ghost. Amen.

IT is in thy name, O adorable Trinity! it is to honor thee, and to do thee homage. that I presume to assist at this most holy and august sacrifice. Permit me then, O Lord! to unite my intention with that of thy minister, in offering up this precious victim; and give me now the sentiments with which I should have been filled, on Mount Calvary, had I been witness to the bloody sacrifice offered thereon..

CONFITEOR

[Think now, in the bitterness of your heart, on all your past sins, and recall to your mind in a general manner, such of them as are most humbling to you. Lay your weakness before God. Beg of him to pardon you, and to assist you in all your necessities, through the infinite merits of this great sacrifice.]

I Confess; O my God! not only in thy presence, who seest the secrets of hearts. but in presence of all the blessed in heaven, and of all the faithful on earth, that I have often and grievously offended thee by my thoughts, words, actions and omissions. Yes, I have sinned, O my God! I have sinned! I acknowledge it to my shame, and with the most bitter regret. I have abused all thy gifts. I am unworthy to appear before thee. But thy mercies, O my God! are above all thy works; thou wilt not despise a contrite, and an humble heart.

O most holy Virgin! and ye angels, and saints of heaven! I humbly beseech you to intercede for me. Vouchsafe, O Lord! to listen to their prayers. Grant to the ardor of their supplication, what thou mayest justly refuse to the coldness of mine; and to their services, so pleasing in thy sight, that pardon, to which my offences can have no claim.

KYRIE ELEISON

[Beg of the Lord to show you mercy, and rely with confidence on his infinite goodness. By granting you so powerful a means of reconciliation as this is, he gives you a sure pledge that you will obtain it.]

THOUGH I were, At every instant of my life, to cry out, Lord, have mercy on me! this would still be unequal to the number and quality of my offences. But though, after long repeating this prayer, thou shouldst appear to disregard me, I would still redouble my importunity, and cry out with a louder and more animated voice, as the woman of Canaan, and the blind man of Jericho did; "Jesus, son of David! have mercy on me!" Be not then tired, O Lord! of my supplications. I know that thou lovest to be importuned. If, as yet, thy goodness hath not granted my pardon, my perseverance shall at length engage thee to grant it. Have pity, bountiful Creator! on the work of thy hands. O Father of mercies! grant pardon to thy children.

GLORIA IN EXCELSIS

[Conceive a great desire of promoting God's glory and your neighbor's good. Rejoice with the angels at the share you have in the holy mysteries, and form to yourself the highest idea of the majesty of God, and of Jesus Christ his Son.]

Gloria in excelsis Deo. Et in terra pax hominibus bonae voluntatis. Laudamus Te. Benedicimus Te. Adoramus Te. Glorificamus Te. Gratias agimus tibi propter magnam gloriam Tuam. Domine Deus, Rex coelestis, Deus Pater omnipotens.

Domine Fili unigenite Iesu Christe. Domine Deus, Agnus Dei, Filius Patris. Qui tollis peccata mundi, miserere nobis. Qui tollis peccata mundi, suscipe deprecationem nostram. Qui sedes ad dexteram Patris, miserere nobis. Quoniam tu solus Sanctus. Tu solus Dominus. Tu solus Altissimus Iesu Christe. Cum Sancto Spiritu in gloria Dei Patris. Amen.

Glory be to God on high, and on earth peace to men of good will. We praise Thee. We bless Thee. We adore Thee. We glorify Thee. We give Thee thanks for Thy great glory. O Lord God, heavenly King, God the Father almighty.

O Lord Jesus Christ, the only begotten Son. O Lord God, Lamb of God, Son of the Father. Thou Who takest away the sins of the world, have mercy on us. Thou Who takest away the sins of the world, receive our prayer. Thou Who sittest at the right hand of the Father, have mercy on us. For Thou only art holy. Thou only art the Lord. Thou only art most high, O Jesus Christ. Together with the Holy Ghost in the glory of God the Father. Amen.

THE COLLECT

[This prayer is so called, because, in it, the priest lays before God the necessities of his people, their vows, and their desires, collected in a manner, together. Whence, turning to the congregation, he says, Oremus, Let as pray, inviting them to unite with him in the petition he is about to make.]

ALMIGHTY, and eternal God! We humbly beseech thee to look down upon this congregation from thy heavenly sanctuary, and graciously hear these prayers of thy Church, addressed to thee for us all, by the ministry of this priest.

Grant us in thy infinite mercy, pardon for our sins, health of mind and body, peace in our days, unity and increase of Catholic Faith, fervor of charity, sincere devotion, patience in suffering, and every thing conducive to thy glory, through Jesus Christ, our Lord. Amen.

THE EPISTLE

[Return God thanks for having called you to the knowledge of his law. Submit to it with perfect docility, and beg him to extend our holy religion over all the world.]

O ETERNAL God! who never ceasest to excite us to the worship, and love of thy holy name, and to arm us against the attacks of the world, the flesh and the devil, by the public ministry of thy Church, by the doctrine of thy prophets and apostles, and by many other holy admonitions, grant we may faithfully attend to these lessons of salvation, that thus our knowledge of thy law may never rise in judgment against us, but guide us securely to thee, through Christ, our Lord. *Amen.*

THE GOSPEL

[Look on the Gospel, which you are now going to hear, as the rule of your faith and morals; a rule which Christ himself has drawn up, which, at your baptism, you have solemnly promised to follow, and by which you shall most certainly be judged.]

IT is not thy interpreters, O God! who are now to instruct me; it is thy only Son; it is his word I am going to hear. I most gratefully embrace this heavenly doctrine. I rise up and declare, in the face of heaven and earth, that I will walk faithfully in that way which he hath marked out for me. He tells me here, "That it will avail a man nothing to gain the whole world, if he lose his own soul; that the sensual, the covetous; the worldling, the libertine, the detractor. and such as are insensible to the miseries of the poor, shall have no share in his heavenly kingdom; and that, in order to become his disciple, I must take up my cross and follow him." I receive, with all my heart, these sacred maxims; grant me the grace to put them in practice. For, to what purpose, O my Jesus! should I declare myself thy disciple, if I were not to live according to thy Gospel!

THE CREED

[Renew here your faith. All these things which the Church proposes to your belief, are founded on God's own word, revealed in the scriptures, announced by the prophets, supported by miracles, confirmed by the martyrs, verified by the establishment of our faith, and obvious by the sanctity of our religion.]

Credo in unum Deum, Patrem omnipotentem, factorem caeli et terrae, visibilium omnium, et invisibilium. Et in unum Dominum Iesum Christum, Filium Dei unigenitum. Et ex Patre natum ante omnia saecula. Deum de Deo, lumen de lumine, Deum verum de Deo vero. Genitum, non factum, consubstantialem Patri: per quem omnia facta sunt. Qui propter nos homines, et propter nostram salutem descendit de coelis. ET INCARNATUS EST DE SPIRITU SANCTO EX MARIA VIRGINE: ET HOMO FACTUS EST. Crucifixus etiam pro nobis: sub Pontio Pilato passus et sepultus est. Et resurrexit tertia die, secundum Scripturas. Et ascendit in Coelum: sedet ad dexteram Patris. Et iterum venturus est cum gloria iudicare vivos, et mortuos: cuius regni non erit finis. Et in Spiritum Sanctum Dominum et vivificantem: qui

I believe in one God, The Father almighty, Maker of heaven and earth, and of all things, visible and invisible. And in one Lord Jesus Christ, the only begotten Son of God. And born of the Father, before all ages. God of God: Light of Light: true God of true God. Begotten, not made, consubstantial with the Father, by whom all things were made. Who, for us men, and for our salvation, came down from Heaven. AND BECAME INCARNATE BY THE HOLY GHOST OF THE VIRGIN MARY: AND WAS MADE MAN. He was crucified also for us, suffered under Pontius Pilate, and was buried. And the third day He rose again according to the Scriptures. And ascended into Heaven, and sitteth at the right hand of the Father. And He shall come again with glory to judge both the living and the dead, of whose kingdom there shall be no end. And in the Holy Ghost, the Lord and Giver of

ex Patre Filioque procedit. Qui cum Patre et Filio simul adoratur, et conglorificatur: qui locutus est per prophetas. Et unam sanctam catholicam et apostolicam Ecclesiam. Confiteor unum baptisma in remissionem peccatorum. Et expecto resurrectionem mortuorem. Et vitam venturi saeculi. Amen.

Life, proceeding from the Father and the Son. Who together, with the Father and the Son, is adored and glorified: Who spoke by the prophets. And in one, holy, Catholic and Apostolic Church. I confess one baptism for the remission of sins. And I look for the resurrection of the dead. And the life of the world to come. *Amen.*

THE OFFERTORY

[Consider what an advantage it is to have, in this great Sacrifice, wherewith to honor God perfectly, to thank him in a manner equal to his gifts, to blot out entirely your past sins, and to obtain, both for yourself and others, all the graces you stand in need of]

O HOLY Father, Almighty and Eternal God! how unworthy soever I be to appear in thy presence, I dare to offer thee this Host, by the hands of the priest, with that intention which Christ my Saviour had, when he first instituted this sacrifice, and which he has, at this very instant, that he immolates himself for us. I offer it in acknowledgment of thy supreme dominion over me, and all creatures. I offer it in expiation of my crimes, and in thanksgiving for all thy benefits. I offer it to obtain of thy infinite goodness, for my parents; benefactors, friends and enemies, all those precious graces, which only through him can be obtained, who is the JUST ONE by excellence, and who became a victim for the sins of men.

Accept then, O Lord! this ineffable sacrifice, as a sweet odor, and permit me to unite to this sacred oblation, the sacrifice of my soul and body, and whatever I am, or have. Change me, O Lord! and make me a new creature in Christ, as thou art going to change this bread and wine by thy power, to make them the body and blood of thy Son.

THE LAVABO

O! WHAT cleanness and purity of heart should we not bring with us to this great sacrifice! But, alas! I am a poor, unclean sinner. Oh wash me, dear Lord! from all the stains of sin in the blood of the Lamb, that I may be worthy to be present at these heavenly mysteries.

THE ORATE FRATRES

RECEIVE, O Lord! from the hands of the priest, the sacrifice which is now prepared, for the praise and the glory of thy name, for our benefit, and that of all thy holy Church. Graciously hear the prayers, which she now offers to thee, by the mouth of her minister, and mercifully grant us all the graces, which thou knowest to be necessary for our salvation.

THE PREFACE

[Raise your thoughts to heaven, to the very throne of the Divinity; and there with most holy and respectful awe, pay homage to his glorious Majesty, mixing your praises with those sacred hymns which the heavenly spirits are ever singing to him.]

V. Dominus vobiscum.

V. The Lord be with you.

R. Et cum spiritu tuo.

R. And with thy spirit.

V. Sursum Corda.

V. Lift up your hearts.

R. Habemus ad Dominum.

V. We have them lifted up to the Lord.

V. Gratias agamus Domino Deo nostro.

V. Let us give thanks to the Lord our God.

R. Dignum et justum est.

V. It is meet and just.

P. Vere dignum et justum est, aequum et salutare, nos tibi semper, et ubique gratias

P. It is truly meet and just, right and available to salvation, that we should

agere: Domine sancte, Pater omnipotens, aeterne Deus. Qui cum unigenito Filio tuo, et Spiritu Sancto, unus es Deus, unus es Dominus: non in unius singularitate personae, sed in unius Trinitate substantiae. Quod enim de tua gloria, revelante te, credimus, hoc de Filio tuo, hoc de Spritu Sancto, sine differentia discretionis sentimus. Ut in confessione verae, sempiternaeque Deitatis, et in personis proprietas, et in essentia unitas, et in majestate adoretur aequalitas. Quam laudant Angeli, atque Archangeli, Cherubim quoque ac Seraphim: qui non cessant clamare quotidie, una voce dicentes:

Sanctus, Sanctus, Sanctus Dominus Deus Sabaoth. Pleni sunt coeli et terra gloria tua. Hosanna in excelsis. Benedictus qui venit in nomine Domini. — Hosanna in excelsis.

always, and in all places give thanks to thee, O holy Lord, Father almighty, eternal God, who with thy only begotten Son and the Holy Ghost, art one God, and one Lord; not in one person, but in three persons and one substance. For what we believe of thy glory, as thou has revealed it, we believe the same of thy Son and of the Holy Ghost, without any difference: so that, in the confession of one true and eternal Deity, we adore a distinction of persons, an unity of essence and an equality of majesty; which the Angels and Archangels praise, the Cherubim and Seraphim also, who cease not to cry out daily saying, with one voice:

Holy! Holy! Holy! Lord God of Sabaoth, the heavens and the earth are full of thy glory. Hosanna in the highest. Blessed is he that cometh in the name of the Lord. Hosanna in the highest.

THE CANON

[Represent here to yourself the altar as a throne of mercy, upon which Christ is to sit, where you are entitled to present yourself, to expose to him your wants, to ask for blessings, and to obtain them. Can he who giveth us his only Son, refuse us any thing!]

O FATHER of mercy! graciously receive by the hands of the priest, this most holy sacrifice, in union with that which thy beloved Son offered up to thee, during his whole life, at his last supper, and on the cross. Look down on thy Christ, thy dearest and only begotten, in whom thou art always well pleased; and by the infinite merits of his Incarnation, of his Nativity, of his tears, labors, sufferings, and death, have mercy upon me, and upon all those for whom I ought to pray, (*here name the particular persons,*) my parents, brethren, friends, benefactors, relations, and those who have injured me, or whom I have injured. I also beseech thee to guard, prosper, and extend the holy Catholic Church, to pour down thy blessing upon our chief pastor the Pope, upon the bishops, and all the clergy; enlighten and guide them in the way of salvation. Bless and preserve our rulers and all our fellow citizens. Look upon us all, I beseech thee, with eyes of mercy and compassion. Bring us all to the perfect practice of a holy, and virtuous life here, and to the possession of thy eternal glory hereafter. May we all know thee; may we all please thee perfectly, may we fear, love and glorify thee, through the same Jesus Christ, who, with thee and the Holy Ghost, liveth and reigneth one God, world without end. A*men.*

Why have I not, O God! at this moment, the ardent sighs with which the holy patriarchs wished for the Messiah? Why have I not their faith, and all their love? Come, Lord Jesus! come, sweet Redeemer of the world! to accomplish a mystery, which is an abridgment of all thy wonders!

Thou art, indeed, the true Pastor of souls, who didst lay down thy life for thy flock. Thou art the Lamb of God, that died upon the cross, to save us. I prostrate myself in spirit before thee, and desire to praise and bless thee for ever.

THE ELEVATION

[Behold your God, your Saviour, and your Judge; remain for a while in silent astonishment at what passes before you; call up all your fervor, and all those sentiments which fear, respect, and confidence can inspire.]

HAIL, Victim of Salvation! Eternal King! Incarnate Word, sacrificed for me and all mankind! Hail, precious body of the Son of God! Hail, sacred flesh, torn with nails, pierced with a lance, and bleeding on a cross, for us poor sinners! O amazing goodness! O infinite love! Oh! let that tender love plead now in my behalf! let all my iniquities be here effaced, and my name be written in the book of life! I believe in thee; I hope in thee; I love thee. To thee, be honor, praise and glory from all creatures for ever.

AT THE ELEVATION OF THE CHALICE

Hail, sacred Blood! flowing from the wounds of Jesus Christ, and washing away the sins of the world! Oh! cleanse, sanctify, and preserve my soul, that nothing may separate me from thee! Behold, O eternal Father! thy holy Jesus; and look upon the face of thy Christ, in whom thou art well pleased. Hear the voice of his blood, that cries out to thee, not for vengeance, but for pardon and mercy. Accept this divine oblation, and through the infinite merits of all that Jesus endured on the cross for our salvation, be pleased to look upon us, and upon all thy people, with an eye of mercy.

THE CANON CONTINUED

[Contemplate, in the most affectionate manner, your Saviour here present. Reflect on the mysteries he here renews; unite the sacrifice of your heart to that of his body; offer him to God his Father, with the several intentions, with which the sacrifice should be offered, beseeching the Father of mercy, to accept the prayers, which his dear Son addresses to him in your behalf.]

IT is now, O Eternal Majesty! that we truly and really offer thee that pure, holy, and immaculate victim, which of thyself thou hast been pleased to grant us, and of which all other offerings were only the types. The sacrifices of Abel, of Abraham, and Melchisedech, were nothing compared to ours. This glorious victim, thy dear Son himself, the perfect object of thy eternal love, is alone worthy of thy altar, and an offering by so much the more precious than theirs. as God is greater than all creatures.

OFFER THE MASS, AS A SACRIFICE OF ADORATION.

O SOVEREIGN Lord of all things! graciously accept my humble homage, in union with that which thou here receivest from Christ, thy beloved Son, in whom thou art well pleased. With him, I offer thee his own holy sacrifice, for the end he proposes, while he immolates himself upon this altar. He alone knows the boundless excellence of thy unspeakable majesty. He alone fully comprehends the entire extent of thy dominion. He beholds thee as thou art; and how all creatures, visible and invisible, depend on thee. He clearly conceives, that thy right is absolute over all we are. and all we possess, or can hope for in this life and in eternity. It is to acknowledge this supreme dominion, and to make in his name a public profession of our total dependence upon thee, that he renews every day, and that we renew with him, this most holy sacrifice.

OFFER IT AS A SACRIFICE OF THANKSGIVING.

VOUCHSAFE also, dearest Lord! to receive this precious victim in thanksgiving for all thy benefits. Thou has created me to thy own likeness, and without thee, I must fall back into my original nothingness. For my sake, thy beloved Son gave himself up to the cruelty of the Jews, and to an ignominious death; nor doth a moment of my existence pass away, without new proofs of thy bounty. I wish, O Lord! I could, even at the price of my blood, acknowledge, in some degree, these numberless favors; but the offering I here make thee, is far more acceptable; it is thy own Son, equal in all things to thee; the figure of thy substance, the splendor of thy glory.

AS A SACRIFICE OF EXPIATION.

REMEMBER, O merciful Father! that the sacrifice we are now offering to thee, is a representation of that, which was offered by our Saviour on the cross. May it be now again a propitiatory sacrifice. Pardon us our ingratitude. Our transgressions, it is true, are grievous and manifold; but then, O Lord! it is the blood of a God we offer in atonement.

AS A SACRIFICE OF IMPETRATION

GOD! who art infinitely bountiful, be pleased now, to crown all thy favors by the gift of a lively faith, of a firm hope, of an ardent charity. Bless all my labors; give me clearly to know thy holy will, and steadily to execute it; grant me to persevere in thy grace to the end of my life. Have mercy on the souls of the faithful departed, and particularly on those, whom I am bound to pray for. [*Name them.*] Deliver them, O Lord! from their sufferings, through the powerful merits of thy Son.

PATER NOSTER

[Here we are with Jesus on a new Calvary. Let us remain at the foot of his cross, with the tender compassion of Magdalen, with the ardent love of St. John; or standing afar off with St. Peter, let us weep bitterly over our offences. With sentiments like these, let us recite the Lord's prayer with the priest.]

PATER NOSTER! qui es in cælis: Sanctificétur nomen tuum: Advéniat regnum tuum. Fiat volúntas tua, sicut in coelo, et in terra. Panem nostrum quotidianum da nobis hodie. Et dimitte nobis debita nostra, sicut et nos dimittimus debitoribus nostris. Et ne nos inducas in tentationem. *R.* Sed líbera nos a malo. *P. Amen.*

OUR FATHER! who art in heaven; hallowed be thy name. Thy kingdom come. Thy will be done on earth as it is in heaven. Give us, this day, our daily bread. And forgive us our trespasses, as we forgive those who trespass against us. And lead us not into temptation; but deliver us from evil. *Amen.*

DELIVER us, we beseech thee, O Lord! from all evils past, present, and to come. And by the intercession of the blessed and ever Virgin Mary, mother of God, and of the holy apostles Peter, Paul, and Andrew, and all the saints, mercifully grant peace in our days, that through the assistance of thy mercy, we may be always free from sin, and secure from all disturbance, through the same Jesus Christ, our Lord, who with thee liveth and reigneth in the unity of the Holy Ghost, world without end. *Amen.*

THE AGNUS DEI

[God, so glorious in heaven, so powerful on earth, so dreadful in hell, is here only, a Lamb full of sweetness and bounty. He comes here to take away the sins of the world, and your sins in particular. What a motive of confidence! What a subject of consolation!]

O LAMB of God! sacrificed for my sake, have mercy on me. O adorable victim of my salvation! look down on me, and save me. Divine Mediator! obtain pardon of thy Father for me, a sinner, and mercifully grant me the sweets of thy peace. Amen.

THE COMMUNION

[To communicate spiritually, renew by an act of Faith, your firm belief of Christ's real presence. Make an act of contrition. Desire most earnestly to receive him with the priest. Beg him to accept these desires, and to unite himself to you in the effusion of his graces.]

WHAT a comfort to me, O my God! were I in the number of those, whose sanctity allows them to receive thee daily! What an advantage, if I could at this instant possess thee in my heart, pay thee there my homage, lay open to thee my wants, and share in the favors, which thou grantest to those who receive thee really! But since I am unworthy, do thou, O Lord! supply my want of dispositions; pardon me my sins; I detest them from my heart, because they are displeasing to thee. Accept my ardent wish to be united to thee; cast thine eye upon me, and purify my soul, that I may soon be fit to receive thee worthily. But, until the arrival of this happy day, I earnestly entreat thee, O dearest Lord! that thou wouldst make me a sharer in all the advantages, which the communion of the priest shall produce in these thy people.

Increase my faith by the virtue of this sacrament, strengthen my hope, refine in my soul thy divine charity, fill my heart with love, that it beat but for thee, and live for thee alone. Amen.

THE LAST PRAYER.

[Strive earnestly to offer your Lord sacrifice for sacrifice, becoming the victim of his love. Immolate freely to him all sinful inclinations, and whatever is contrary to his holy will.]

THOU hast offered thyself, O Lord! for my salvation; I desire to be sacrificed for thy glory. I am thy victim; do with me as thou willest. Whatever I have, I consecrate entirely to thee. Those crosses, which thou shalt please to send me, I most freely accept. I bless them; I receive them from thy hand, and unite them with those thou hast endured for my sake. I am now about to leave thy temple, resolved, with thy help, to serve thee faithfully. I will struggle against my failings, but chiefly against that to which I am most inclined. Thy law shall henceforth direct me, and I shall forfeit all, and suffer every thing, rather than mortally transgress it.

THE BENEDICTION

[Receive this blessing from the priest, as being given you in the name of the Lord. Thank him sincerely for the favors here granted you; lay up with care the fruits of this sacrifice, and let your conduct be such, that all who see you, may clearly perceive how much you have profited by so holy an action.]

MOST holy and adorable Trinity! by thee we have begun this sacrifice, by thee we desire to conclude it; we therefore shall not leave thee, until thou bless us. Give us. O Lord! thy blessing, by the hands of this priest; may it ever remain with us; may it influence our actions, and be the sure pledge of that last benediction, which thy elect shall receive, when called by thee into eternal glory.

THE LAST GOSPEL

DIVINE Word, only Son of the Father, Light of the world! who earnest from heaven to show us the way to it, I adore thy Majesty with the most profound respect. I place my whole confidence in thee. I hope most firmly, that as thou art my God, a God made man to save mankind, thou wilt grant me those graces my sanctification requires. and also the enjoyment of thee in thy glory.

A PRAYER AFTER MASS

I EARNESTLY thank thee, O my God! for having permitted me to assist at the celebration of this holy sacrifice, in preference to so many others; who have not been thus favored. I humbly entreat thee to pardon me the faults, which I have committed during it, either by my inattention or my neglect. Grant that I remember through the course of the day, what thou hast here done for me. Grant that no thought, word; or action of mine, deprive me of the graces, of which, through thy infinite mercy, I have been partaker.

The manner of serbing and answering at Mass

[The clerk, or minister, kneeling at the left hand of the priest, shall answer him, as follows:]

Priest. INTROIBO ad Altare Dei.

Clerk. Ad Deum qui laetificat juventutem meam.

P. Judica me, Deus, et discerne causam meam de gente non sancta: ab homine iniquo et doloso erue me.

C. Quia tu es Deus, fortitudo mea: quare me repulisti, et quare tristis incedo, dum affligit me inimicus?

P. Emitte lucem tuam et veritatem tuam: ipsa me deduxerunt, et adduxerunt in montem sanctum tuum, et in tabernacula tua.

C. Et introibo ad altare Dei: ad Deum, qui lætificat juventutem meam.

P. Confitebor tibi in cithara, Deus, Deus meus: quare tristis es, anima mea, et quare conturbas me?

C. Spera in Deo, quoniam adhuc confitebor illi: salutare vultus mei, et Deus meus.

P. Gloria Patri, et Filio, et Spiritui Sancto.

C. Sicut erat in principio, et nunc, et semper: et in sæcula sæculorum. Amen.

P. Introibo ad altare Dei.

C. Ad Deum qui laetificat juventutem meam.

P. Adjutorium nostrum in nomine Domini.

C. Qui fecit coelum et terram.

P. Confiteor Deo, &c.

C. Misereatur tui omnipotens Deus, et dimissis peccatis tuis, perducat te ad vitam aeternam.

P. Amen.

C. Confíteor Deo omnipotenti, beatæ Maríæ semper Vírgini, beáto Michaeli Archangelo, beato Joanni Baptistæ, Sanctis Apostolis Petro et Paulo, omnibus Sanctis, et tibi, Pater, quia peccavi nimis cogitatione, verbo, et opere (*here strike your breast thrice,*) mea culpa, mea culpa, mea maxima culpa. Ideo precor beatam Mariam semper Virginem, beatum Michaelem Archangelum, beatum Joannem Baptistam, Sanctos Apostolos Petrum et Paulum, omnes Sanctos, et te, Pater, orare pro me ad Dominum Deum nostrum.

P. Misercatur vestri, &c.

C. Amen.

P. Indulgentiam, absolutionem, et remissionem, &c.

C. Amen.

P. Deus to conversus, vivificabis nos.

C. Et plebs tua laetabitur in te.

P. Ostende nobis, Domine, misericordiam tuam.

C. Et salutare tuum da nobis.

P. Domine, exandi orationem meam. a Et clamor mews ad te veniat.

P. Dominus vobiscum.

C. Et cum spiritu tuo.

[After the *Introit*, the priest returns to the middle of the altar and says]

P. Kyrie eleison.

C. Kyrie eleison.

P. Kyrie eleison.

C. Christe eleison.

P. Christe eleison.

C. Christe eleison.

P. Kyrie eleison.

C. Kyrie eleison.

P. Kyrie eleison.

P. Dominus vobiscum.

C. Et cum spiritu tuo.

[When the priest says, Flectamus genus.. The C. *answers*, Levate.]

P. Per omnia saecula saeculorum.

C. Amen.

[At the end of the Epistle, say:]

C. Deo gratias.

[The *Epistle, Gradual* and *Alleluia* or *Tract*, being read, remove the Mass-book to the right corner of the altar, making a reverence, as you pass before the middle of the altar. Always kneel or stand on the side opposite to that on which the book is placed.]

P. Dominus vobiscum,

C. Et cum spiritu tuo.

P. Sequentia sancti Evangelii secundum, &c.

[Making the sign of the cross on your forehead, mouth and breast, and bowing, say:]

C. Gloria tibi, Domino!

[Always bow at the name of Jesus. At the end of the Gospel, say:]

C. Laus tibi, Christe!

P. Dominus vobiscum.

C. Et cum spiritu tuo.

[When the priest has offered the bread, the clerk gives him wine and water; then prepares the towel, and gives him water for his hands That done, let him kneel down as before.]

P. Orate, fratres.

C. Suscipiat Dominus Sacrificium de manibus tuis, ad laudem et gloriam nominis sui, ad utilitatem quoque nostram, totiusque Ecclesiae suae sanctae.

P. Per omnia saecula saeculorum.

C. Amen.

P. Dominus Vobiscum.

C. Et cum spiritu tuo.

P. Sursum corda.

C. Habemus ad Dominum.

P. Gratias agamus Domino Deo nostro.

C. Dignum et justum est.

[At *Sanctus, Sanctus, Sanctus*, ring the little bell. When you see the priest spread his hands over the chalice, you mast give warning, by the bell, of the consecration, which is about to be made. Light the candle, if any be prepared for that purpose. Then holding up the vestment with your left hand, with the right, ring the bell during the elevation of the host. Do the same at the elevation of the chalice. As often as you pass by the blessed Sacrament, make a genuflexion.]

P. Per omnia saecula saeculorum.

C. Amen.

P. Et ne nos inducas in tentationem.

C. Sed libera nos a malo.

P. Per omnia saecula saeculorum.

C. Amen.

P. Pax Domini sit semper vobiscum.

C. Et cum spiritu tuo

[The priest's communion being ended, be ready to give him wine first, then wine and water. But if there be any communicants, provide first a communion cloth, and say the *Confiteor*. And after the communion, give the priest wine and water. Then remove the book to the left corner of the altar, put out the candle which you lighted before the elevation, take away the communion cloth, and return to your former place.]

P. Dominus vobiscum.

C. Et cum spiritu tuo.

P. Per omnia saecula saeculorum.

C. Amen.

P. Ite, Missa est, *or* Benedicamus Domino.

C. Deo gratias.

[In *Masses* for the dead. *P*. Requiescant in pace. *C*. Amen.]

[If the book be left open, remove it. Kneel to receive the priest's blessing.]

P. Pater et Filius et Spiritus Sanctus.

C. Amen.

P. Dominus vobiscum.

C. Et cum spiritu tuo.

P. Initium *or* sequentia sancti Evangelii secundum &c.

C. Gloria tibi, Domine.

[At the end of the last gospel, whatever it may be, say: Deo Gratias.]

Devotions before Confession

A PRAYER BEFORE CONFESSION

O ALMIGHTY and most merciful God! who hast made me out of nothing, and redeemed me by the precious blood of thy only Son; who hast borne with me to this day with so much patience, notwithstanding my sins and ingratitude; behold me, O Lord! prostrate at thy feet to implore thy forgiveness. I desire most sincerely to leave all my evil ways, to forsake this region of death where I have so long lost myself, and to return to thee, the fountain of life. I desire, like the prodigal child, to enter seriously into myself. and, with the like resolutions, to rise without delay, and go home to my Father, though I am infinitely unworthy to be called his child, in hopes of meeting with the like reception from his most tender mercy. I know thou desirest not the death of a sinner, but that he may be converted and live. I know thy mercies are above all thy works; and 1 most confidently hope, that as in thy mercy thou hast spared me so long, and hast now given me this desire of returning to thee, so thou wilt finish the work thou hast begun, and bring me to a perfect reconciliation with thee.

I desire now to comply with thy holy institution of the sacrament of penance. I desire to confess my sins with all sincerity to thee and to thy minister, and therefore I desire to know myself and to call myself to an account by a diligent examination of my conscience.

But, O my good God! what will it avail me to know my sins, if thou dost not also give me a hearty sorrow and repentance for them. Without this, my sins will be all against me still, and I shall be still thy enemy and a child of hell. Thou insistest upon a change of heart, without which there can be no reconciliation with thee; and this change of heart none but thou canst give. Oh! give it me then, dear Lord! at this time. Give me a lively faith and a firm hope in the passion of my Redeemer. Teach me to fear thee, and to love thee. Give me, for thy mercy's sake, a hearty sorrow for having offended so good a God.

O blessed Virgin, mother of my Redeemer, mirror of innocence and sanctity, and refuge of penitent sinners! intercede for me through the passion of thy Son, that I may obtain the grace to make a good confession. O all you blessed angels and saints of God! pray for me, a most miserable sinner, that I may now effectually turn from my evil ways, that my heart may henceforward be for ever united with yours in eternal love, and never more go astray from the sovereign good. *Amen.*

A SHORT TABLE OF SINS:

To help the memory when we prepare for Confession.

AGAINST THE COMMANDMENTS

1. Have you doubted in matters of faith?

Murmured against God at your own adversary, or at the prosperity of others Despaired of his mercy?

Believed in fortune-tellers, or consulted them?

Gone to places of worship belonging to other denominations?

Not recommended yourself daily to God?

2. Taken the name of God in vain?

Spoken irreverently of holy things, or profaned any thing relating to religion?

Sworn falsely, rashly, or in slight and trivial matters?

Cursed yourself, or others, or any creature?

Angered others so far as to make them swear, or blaspheme God?

3. Have you kept holy the Lord's day, and all other days commanded to be kept holy?

Bought or sold things, not of necessity for that day?

Done or commanded some servile work, not of necessity?

Missed Mass, or been willfully distracted in time of Mass?

Talked, gazed, or laughed in the church.

Profaned the day by dancing, drinking, gambling? &c.

4. Have you honored your parents, superiors, masters, according to your just duty?

Deceived them; disobeyed them? Failed in due reverence to aged persons?

5. Procured, desired, or hastened the death of any one?

Borne hatred; oppressed any; desired revenge; not forgiven; refused to speak to others; given provoking language; threatened or struck others not under your charge; made others fall out?

6 & 9. Have you been guilty of lascivious dressing or painting; lewd company; have you read immodest books? been guilty of unchaste songs, discourses, words, looks, or actions by yourself or others? Willfully entertained impure thoughts or desires?

7. Stealing; deceit in gaming, reckoning, buying or selling, in wares, prices, weights, or measures; bought of such as could not sell; willfully damaged another man's goods, or negligently

spoiled them; run into debt carelessly, beyond your power of payment?

Borne false witness; called injurious names; uttered another's sins; Flattered yourself or others; opened others' letters; judged rashly; falsely suspected?

10. Coveted unjustly any thing that belongs to another?

Precepts of the Church. — Have you gone to confession, at least once a year? received the holy communion during the Easter-time?

Have you not violated the fasts of the Church, or eaten flesh-meat on prohibited days?

The Seven Capital Sins. — Pride, Covetousness, Luxury, Anger, Gluttony, Envy, Sloth.

AFFECTIONS AND RESOLUTIONS BEFORE CONFESSION

MY Lord, and my all! I am confounded at the multitude and enormity of my offences against so good a God. I dare not presume even to lift up my eyes to heaven, much less to come near thy altar, after so many treasons against thee. Alas! what shall I now do, O Lord! What shall I say? With the humble publican I will strike my breast, and cry unto thee; O *God! be merciful to me, a sinner.*

My sins exceed in number the hairs of my head, and the sands of the sea. But thy mercies are still greater in number than my sins. O ocean of mercy! have compassion on me, a poor miserable sinner, and make me, now at last, a true penitent.

Father, I have sinned against heaven, and in thy sight, and am not worthy to be called thy child. Oh! receive me as one of the least of thy servants, and never suffer me to stray from thee any more.

It grieves me, O my God I that I have offended thee. I am heartily sorry for all the sins I have committed against thy infinite goodness: Oh! that I could sufficiently lament them, even with tears of blood.

Who will give water to my head, and fountains of tears to my eyes, that, night and day, I may bewail all my sins and my ingratitude!

Oh! that I had never offended my God! Oh! that I had never sinned! happy those souls, who have never lost their baptismal innocence! Ah! sweet Jesus! that I had been so happy!

Have mercy on me, O God! according to thy great mercy, and according to the multitude of thy tender mercies, blot out all my iniquities. Wash me yet more from my iniquities, and cleanse me from my sins; because I know my iniquities, and my sins are always before me.

Oh! that I could now, like Magdalen, prostrate myself at the feet of my Saviour! Oh! that I could wash them with my tears! Oh! suffer me, dear Lord! to lay down all my sins at thy feet, to be cancelled by thy precious blood.

Lord! thou hast said, there is joy in heaven upon one sinner's doing penance, more than upon ninety-nine just: Oh! give me now grace to be a true penitent, indeed, that hereby heaven may rejoice at my conversion.

Thou earnest, O my dear Redeemer! not to call the just, but sinners, to repentance. Look down upon me, a poor miserable sinner, and draw me now powerfully to thee by thy grace.

I know thou willest not the death of a sinner, but that he be converted, and live. Oh! let me no longer remain dead in my sins! Oh! let me now at least begin to live to thee!

Create a clean heart in me, O God! and renew a right spirit within my bowels. Oh! grant that I may now serve thee in good earnest! Let this be the change of the right hand of the Most High!

Thou hast made me, O my God! and redeemed me by thy precious blood. Oh! despise not the work of thy hands, and let not thy blood be spilt for me in vain!

Too late have I known thee, O eternal truth! too late have I loved thee, O eternal beauty! too long have I gone astray from thee! From this moment, O my Sovereign Good! I desire to be for ever thine. Oh! let nothing, in life or death, ever separate me from thee any more!

O divine lover of penitent souls! give me henceforth a contrite and humble heart. I wish from this hour to offer this sacrifice to thee daily, to the end of my life.

O divine love, how little art thou known in this wicked world! how little art thou loved! Come now, and take full possession of my whole heart and soul, for time and eternity.

Thy mercy has been infinite, in bearing so long with so ungrateful a sinner as I have been, and in daily heaping thy favors upon me. Add this one favor, O Lord! to all the rest, that henceforth, through thy grace, I may never offend thee more. This one thing I earnestly beg of thee, for thy infinite mercy's sake, and through the death and passion of thy only Son. Hear this one prayer, I beseech thee, and in all things else do with me what thou pleasest.

I am resolved, by thy grace, never more to turn to my sins. Oh! rather let me die than offend thee willfully any more. I am resolved to avoid all evil company, and dangerous occasions; and to take proper measures for a thorough amendment of my life for the future. All this I resolve; but thou knowest my frailty, O my God! and if thou assist me not with they grace, all my resolution will prove ineffectual, and I shall be for ever miserable. Oh! look to me, O Lord! that I may never betray thee any more.

METHOD OF CONFESSING

After having carefully examined your conscience, excited yourself to a hearty sorrow for your sins, and made a firm purpose of amendment, go and make your confession to the minister of God, who, in virtue of the power and commission which he has received to that effect, is, either "to forgive or retain, to loose or bind," according to the preparation of your heart, the nature of your transgressions, their number, their enormity, &c.

In going to confession, humble yourself by considering the majesty of God, and your own many infirmities and great unworthiness. Let your confession be plain, entire, and prudent; neither obscuring your faults, nor concealing any thing willfully, nor saying what would be prejudicial to a third person.

Being on your knees, in the attitude of a suppliant, say first: Bless me, Father, because I have sinned; "I confess to Almighty God," &c., p. 11, as far as "through my fault."

Then proceed thus: Since my last confession, which was (*mention the time*) I accuse myself of, &c. &c.

Having finished the declaration of your sins, add: For these and all other sins that have escaped my memory, I am heartily sorry, humbly ask pardon of God, and penance and absolution of you, my ghostly father, "through my fault," &c.

After this, listen attentively to the instructions and advice of your confessor, answer his questions, and humbly accept the penance which he will enjoin. Whilst he absolves you, bow down your head, and, with profound humility, say

AN ACT OF CONTRITION

O MY God! I am most heartily sorry for all my sins; and I detest them above all things, because they displease thee, who art infinitely good and amiable, and subject me to the rigors of thy justice; and I firmly resolve, with the help of thy grace, to do penance for them, and never more to offend thee.

Prayers after Confession

Ⓞ God of infinite goodness! who hast shown such mercy to a miserable sinner! O most indulgent Father! who hast received once more thy prodigal child. how shall I thank thee? how shall I testify the joy and gratitude that fill my heart? O that I could worthily thank thee, my good God! and acknowledge, as I ought, that infinite mercy which *forgiveth all my iniquities, which healeth all my diseases*. Ps. 102:3. Oh! that I could now be heard all over the world, I would publish to all sinners, that thou art a God *compassionate and merciful, who wilt not always be angry, nor threaten for ever*. Ibid. 8, 9. I would invite all who ever had the misfortune of offending thee, to return with their whole hearts. that they may enjoy with me the bliss of having been received into thy grace and favor. Thou wouldst receive them no less mercifully than thou receivedst me; *for as a father hath compassion on his children, so hath the Lord compassion on them that fear him*. Ibid. 13. My God, thou hast broken the bonds of my sins; thou hast blotted out, with thy own precious blood, the sentence of eternal death, which stood against me; thou hast snatched me almost from the brink of hell, and delivered me from the power of the devil, who has now no claim to my soul: *as far as the east is from the west, so far host thou removed my iniquities from me*, (lb. 12.) and by the mouth of thy minister thou hast desired the most unworthy of all sinners to *"Go in peace."* O divine Jesus! I have obeyed thy command, my heart rejoices, my soul is truly at peace, because I hope I am no longer thy enemy; because thou hast received me with mercy and forgiveness, and satisfied the first and only desire of my heart. But, Lord! hast thou not said, that those to whom much has been forgiven, should love thee much? To whom hast thou ever remitted such ingratitude as mine? who had ever so little claim on thy compassion; yet, at the same time, who ever experienced more of thy mercy and goodness? Oh! let me then love thee, at least, more than those who offended thee less, and to whom less was remitted; let me love thee unceasingly, and sincerely begin, from this happy day, to serve thee alone, and love thee above all created things. O most bountiful Redeemer, so worthy of my whole heart! though thou hast mercifully forgiven me, yet I will never pardon myself; though I firmly trust thou hast forgotten my iniquities, yet I will never forget them, but grieve over them to the last moment of my life. The more mercy and tenderness I have experienced from thee, the more reason I have to deplore my misfortune in having ever offended so good a God. This day shall be the beginning of my perfect conversion; from this moment forward, the recollection of my past ingratitude and thy ineffable goodness shall be ever present to my mind, and with the assistance of thy grace, shall be a double motive for detesting sin, and faithfully observing my resolutions, which I fervently renew, and once more present to thy divine Majesty. Do not refuse to receive, O my God! the remainder of my life. I am heartily sorrowful for the years I have misspent; they have gone down as a shadow; they have passed away without fruit; but as I cannot recall them. I will at least think of them in the bitterness of my soul. Oh! let the ardor with which I pursued a life of sin, be to future applied to thy service, that where sin hath abounded, thy divine grace may be still more abundant. Let the change in my conduct be visible to all, and may I henceforward edify more than I have hitherto scandalized.

O DIVINE Lord! vouchsafe graciously to remember thy holy thoughts from all eternity, and chiefly that tender design of becoming man for the redemption of the world. Pardon me, through the merits of these, all my vain and evil imaginations, as well as the bad thoughts I may have excited in others.

O most compassionate Jesus! I, a wretched sinner, dare to present thee all the words of salvation which have fallen from thy sacred lips, and which others have uttered, or shall hereafter utter to the glory of thy name; and I earnestly beseech thee, through these expressions, full of glory to God and peace to men, to forgive whatever I have said offensive to thy divine Majesty, or what others, through my means, may have sinfully uttered.

O most amiable Lord, Jesus Christ! remember all the good works thou hast performed for our salvation, and through their infinite merits graciously pardon my reiterated offenses against thy holy law. Mercifully direct, all my thoughts, words, and actions to thy greater glory, and regulate them by the model of thy own blessed life.

O JESUS CHRIST, Saviour of the world! who invitest the sinner to return to thee, kindly receiving, refreshing,. and consoling him; remember that with thy precious blood thou wast pleased to redeem my sinful soul: to thy sacred wounds I therefore flee for refuge; and as in thy mercy thou didst pray for thy enemies, and sacrifice thy life for thy tormentors, vonchsafe to impart to me the benefits of thy sacred death and passion. Grant that I may never again crucify thee by any willful offence; but sincerely grieving for the. past, and resolutely striving against present temptations, I may fervently persevere to the end in thy love and service. Into thy hands I commend my whole being. O Jesus, Son of David! have mercy on me.

O HOLY VIRGIN, and all ye saints and angels! bless and extol the Lord for his infinite mercies: beg of him to accept the confession I have made, to supply, through his goodness, for all its deficiencies, and graciously to confirm in heaven the sentence of absolution which has been pronounced upon me on earth.

[For satisfaction (besides your performance of the penance which is enjoined,) you must labor to conquer all inclinations to the sins you have confessed. If you have injured any, you must make restitution as far as you are able; if, by your example or otherwise. you have given scandal or occasion for sin, you must, by contrary virtues. endeavor to repair the spiritual damage of your neighbor.]

Devotions before Communion

[IMAGINE that our Saviour invites you into the same room in which he ate his last supper with his apostles, to be a witness of the miracle he is there going to perform, and to give you communion with his own sacred hands. How fervent soever your sentiments might have been on that solemn occasion, they ought not to be less so at present; for as he ordained that this divine food should be daily renewed, for the nourishment of the faithful, till his second coming to judge mankind at the end of the world, so he gives himself no less to us at present, than he did at that time to his apostles. Take them now for your model. The accounts which we have in the gospel of this last mysterious supper, will furnish you with proper Acts for Communion. Read them attentively: make them your own, by reflection; and let them sink deeply into your heart.]

AN ACT OF ADORATION.

COULD we ever believe, O Lord, or even imagine, that thy love for us was so excessive, had not thine own infallible word convinced us of its truth? hadst thou, when thou wast about to quit this world, left us thy adorable heart as a pledge of thy affection; or hadst thou, when thy side was pierced, ordered thy precious blood to be distributed throughout thy Church; such favors would justly claim our most grateful acknowledgments. But this would not satisfy the extent of thy love: thou didst choose, in a godlike manner, to penetrate into the very centre of our hearts, and give thyself to each of us in particular, entirely, and forever. With what amazement, then, must not the angels, and the whole hierarchy of celestial intelligences, have beheld such a prodigy! Were they not, in some measure, jealous to see mankind thus uncommonly favored? But what didst thou discover in me, O Lord, that could thus attract thee? or what couldst thou possibly expect from my indigence? Can I become the dwelling place of Him who is the delight of the blessed. Alas! had I even the innocence of the beloved disciple St. John, or the ardent love of thy zealous apostle St. Peter, I should then have some little claim to sit down at thy table; but since I am removed at so great a distance from such holy dispositions, vouchsafe, O Lord, to supply my deficiency by the effusion of thy grace. Whence is this favor to me, O my merciful Redeemer? What is man, that thou, art mindful of him? or the son of man, that thou visitest him? Ps. 7:5.

AN ACT OF DESIRE

SINCE thou, O Lord, art so prodigal of miracles, and obligest me to receive thee under such severe penalties, nothing can be more certain than that thou desirest to make my heart thy dwelling place. With what fervent desires should I not, therefore, endeavor to cooperate with intentions so bountiful, O my all-sufficient God! Though thou standest in no need of me, yet thou hast compassion on my poverty. May then the efficacy of thy grace supply my indigence; may it awaken every faculty of my soul, and render my desires to receive thee worthily, still more inflamed: for though they are arrived at a certain anxiety, I am nevertheless sensible of their being too tepid. Alas, my Redeemer! why do I not sigh after thee, with the same holy fervor as did the Patriarchs of the Old Law, who expected thy coming? *Come, O Lord and do not delay*. Remember, O heavenly Physician! that thou canst not refuse thy all-healing balsam to the wounds of my soul, since thy motive for descending on earth was to heal the sins of men. Although I am needy and poor, yet thou canst enrich me. Although I am enslaved under the tyranny of my predominant passions, yet thou canst break my chains and set me at liberty: a single word of thine would be altogether sufficient to work these miracles in favor of one so unworthy of thy corporeal presence as I am. Speak it then, O Sovereign Good! for I can no longer live without thee. Let blind and infatuated worldings intoxicate themselves with the false, transient, and fading happiness of this life; as for my part, nothing besides thyself can content me, either in heaven or on earth; for what have I in heaven, or what can I desire on earth, beside thee? Come, then, O thou Lamb of God, who takest away the sins of the world! Come! thou beloved of my heart! adorable flesh and precious blood of my Saviour! Come, to nourish, comfort, and enliven my sickly soul. O God of my heart! let me neither love, seek, nor think on any other object but thyself alone; for thou alone art my consolation, my treasure, my joy, my life, my God, and my all! My heart as eagerly desires to receive thee, as the wearied stag longs to quench his thirst in the fountains of water.

AN ACT OF FEAR

IF the uncertainty of being worthy of thy love or hatred, O Lord! made even St. Paul, that vessel of election, tremble, how much more reason have not I to apprehend lest some concealed sin, lurking in my heart, might obstruct the salutary influence of those graces, which thou hast prepared for them that worthily receive thee in this divine Sacrament? May not I perhaps, like another Judas, give thee the kiss of peace today, and basely betray thee tomorrow? or, instead of coming to visit me, as a faithful disciple, dost then not rather come with horror and indignation, as to a concealed enemy? How can I answer for the integrity of my confession, the fervor of my contrition, or the sincerity of my resolutions? Is it not custom, or human respect, that brings me to the foot of thy altar? Have I not still some favorite attachment? and in the resolution I have made of relinquishing my evil habits, have I not spared some favorite, though dangerous passion? With the same heartfelt anguish as thy disciples experienced on the like occasion, I ask thee, O Lord! Is it I?

But the most abominable traitor Judas asked thee the same question. Is not my anxiety, as his was, only false and apparent? It is this thought, O my God! that terrifies me; and it is to thyself alone I have recourse to preserve me from so horrible a sacrilege. No; thou wilt never permit me to be guilty of so horrid a profanation, since thou seest there is no evil I dread so much. Wherefore, my dear Saviour! after being as diligent as I could in My preparation to receive thee, I now rest entirely on thy infinite mercy. *Depart from me; for I am a sinful man; Lord!* Luke 5:8. *Son be of good heart; thy sins are forgiven thee.* Matt. 9:2.

AN ACT OF CONTRITION

To transform a soul so defiled as mine into a state of innocence and purity, must be the work of the right hand of the Most High. Ah, my God! I shall never be, able to discover any vestige of that precious innocence which makes a soul so lovely and acceptable in thy sight, unless I trace back my whole life to the days of my childhood. But although I have had the misfortune to forfeit my baptismal innocence by sin, yet there remains for my consolation this sure anchor, whereby I may hope to regain thy favor; grounded on thy infallible promise, viz. *That thou wilt never despise a contrite and humble heart.*

But if even the enormity of my sins had not exposed me to thy wrath, and consequently to the eternal pains of hell, yet would I nevertheless sincerely detest them. O My God! do not upbraid me with mine iniquities, they are always in my sight; and the bitterness of my regret for having committed them, shall serve as a continual punishment of my baseness. Ah, my Redeemer! though I cannot suffer such an excessive degree of anguish as thou didst during thy agony in the garden of Gethsemani, when in a bloody sweat, thou didst offer thyself as a victim to the eternal Father; yet I am fully determined to suffer with patience every cross or affliction which may fall in my way, as well in atonement for the sins I have hitherto commuted, as to prevent me from future relapses. Assist me with thy grace, O bountiful Saviour! and remove every occasion of sin from me; and as I dread no evil so much as that of offending thee, rather cut the thread of my life, than suffer rue again to commit a deliberate sin. O my amiable Saviour! inflamed with thy love, I am fully resolved to avoid every fault that may in the least displease thee; or diminish the influence of thy graces. Although I have a well-grounded confidence that my soul has been cleansed in the Sacrament of Penance, still I desire to be washed more and more front my iniquities. *Create a clean heart in me, O God! and renew a right spirit within my bowels.* Psalm 50:12.

AN ACT OF HUMILITY

WHAT am I, O God of majesty and glory, or who am I that thou shouldst deign even to look on me? Whence am I honored with so unspeakable a favor, as that my Lord and my God should come and visit in person so miserable a sinner and vile a worm of the earth? How. dares a being more contemptible than nothing, approach so holy a God, eat the bread of angels, and feed on thy divine flesh? Ah, Lord! it is too much: I am not worthy of so great a favor; I shall never, no, never deserve it.

O King of heaven and earth! adorable Sovereign! the Author and Preserver of the universe! behold, I annihilate myself before thee, protesting that I would humble myself as much for thy glory, as thou dost here for my salvation. I acknowledge, with the most profound respect, the infinite grandeur of thy divine Majesty, and my own miserable baseness. The contemplation of the one and the other fills me with inexpressible confusion. Can I possibly do more, my dear Saviour! than to confess with the utmost humility, in the words of the Centurion, *Lord! I am not worthy that thou shouldst enter under my roof; but only say the word, and my soul shall be healed.*

AN ACT OF FAITH

SINCE thou, omnipotent God! whose almighty words are creative, productive, and effective; since thou, O eternal Truth! who canst neither deceive nor be deceived; since thou, I say, hast declared that thou art *really* and *actually* present, under the appearance of material bread, I therefore implicitly believe it; for what greater proof can I require of the truth of this mystery, than thine own infallible word? Yes, my dear Saviour, I openly confess, and am inwardly convinced, that it is thou thyself I am going to receive; thou who, for my sake, wast born in a manger; thou who, for my redemption, didst die on a cross, and who, though now gloriously seated on thy heavenly throne, still continuest on earth under the sacramental veils, to feed and nourish the souls of men. Were I to behold thee with my corporal eyes, and examine the impressions of the wounds thou didst receive in thy sacred hands and side, as St. Thomas did, still could not say with more confidence than I now do, that thou art *my Lord and my God.* I do not ask a miracle, as a proof of thy real presence: no, Lord! let me rather have the whole merit of faith; for thou hast said: *Blessed are they that have not seen, and have believed.* Wast thou therefore to speak to me from this very tabernacle. thy voice would affect me less than that which resounds in thy Gospel, and in thy Church founded by thyself and propagated in a miraculous manner. Though to my senses it appears to be bread, yet submitting them entirely in obedience to divine faith, I answer, it is thy real body and blood. accompanied by thy soul and divinity. In this faith I am determined to live and die; and were I to suffer a thousand martyrdoms in testimony thereof, I am persuaded that, with the help of thy grace, I would remain immoveable. *Verily thou art a hidden God, the God of Israel the Saviour.* Is. 45. *I do believe, O Lord; help thou my unbelief.*

AN ACT OF HOPE

SINCE thou vouchsafest to come and dwell within me, O my Redeemer, what may I not expect from thy bounty? I therefore present myself before thee with that lively confidence which thy infinite goodness inspires. Thou not only knowest all my wants, but thou art also willing and able to relieve them. Thou hast not only invited me, but also promised me thy gracious assistance: *Come to me, all you that labor and are heavy laden, and I will refresh you.* Behold, then, O Lord! I accept thy gracious invitation: I lay before thee all my wants, my misery, and my blindness; and confidently hope, without the fear of being disappointed, that thou wilt enlighten my understanding, inflame my will, comfort me in the midst of such crosses or afflictions as thou hast appointed I should suffer, strengthen me in all temptations and trials, and, with the powerful assistance of thy grace, change me into a new creature; for, art not thou, O God, the master of my heart? and when shalt my heart be more absolutely disposed of by thee, than when thou shalt have once entered into it?

Devotions after Communion

AN ACT OF FAITH AND ADMIRATION

Is it credible then, O my soul! that the great God of
heaven and earth should dwell in me? That I should now possess within myself, the same Jesus, who is sitting in heaven at
the right hand of God, and who is there the joy of saints and
angels? Yes, O my Saviour! I firmly believe it. It is thou, O
God of glory! who art hidden under these Sacramental veils,
whom I have just now received, and who dost, at this instant,
reside within me. It is thou, O sovereign Majesty! who
vouchsafest to heap thy favors on me, who am but dust and
ashes, and come into this poor cottage, this house of clay of my
earthly habitation. O heavenly manna! O adorable sacrament! O
inestimable pledge of God's love to mankind! O inexhaustible
fountain of divine grace! O boundless mercy! O divine charity!
O Lord, my God! What is man, that thou art mindful of him; or
the son of man, that thou visitest him! O how sweet, and mild,
and merciful art thou, to those who call upon thee! When I had
no being at all, thou createdst me; when I was gone astray, and
lost in my sins,. thou didst seek after me, and redeem me by
dying for my sake; and after restoring me to life, with more
than a mother's love, thou didst. feed me with thy own
substance, even with thy own flesh and blood! O wonderful
condescension! O immense love bestowed on sinful man!

AN ACT OF ADORATION

UNDER these sacred veils, where thy love for man has
concealed the splendor of thy Majesty, I most humbly adore
thee, O Almighty God! The grandeur of the heavens is in thy
sight as nothing: the heavens are the work of thy hands, O they
shall perish, but thou shalt remain; they shall grow old and be
changed as a garment, but thou art the same and thy years shall
not fail. The earth thou hast poised in thy hand, the ocean is to
thee, but a drop of water; all nature bends before thee, and
trembles in thy presence. How then shall I extol thee, immortal
King of Ages! What homage can I give, proportioned to thy

greatness! Thou art the perfect image of thy Father's substance; thou art the inherent splendor of his glory; thou art his powerful word, supporting all things; thee he hath seated at his right hand. Thy throne, O God! is for ever and ever; a sceptre of justice is the sceptre of thy reign. I bow before thy sacred Majesty; I acknowledge with the sincerest gratitude, that thou art my Redeemer, my Creator, and the supreme Arbiter of my eternal doom. I wish to humble myself as much for thy sake, as thou art here humbled for love of me, and to consecrate to the glory of thy name, the whole extent of my being. O Jesus! be now the absolute Lord and master of my heart. Reign there as a sovereign Monarch on thy throne; rule with an absolute sway over all the powers of my soul. Suffer not the devil, or the world, to have any part in me. Subdue my rebellious nature; deliver me from the shameful slavery of my passions, and grant me the glorious liberty of thy children. O sweet empire of my God! O delightful service of Jesus! To serve thee, O amiable King! is to reign.

AN ACT OF LOVE

AM I then, my God! so happy as to possess thee! What a blessing is this! what unspeakable comfort! Thou art indeed my Saviour; thy goodness hath no bounds; thy beauty is inexpressible; thou art the brightness of eternal light; the glory of heaven is from thee. Thou art the unfailing source of endless happiness; the angels desire to behold thee; thou fillest the hearts of the blessed. Therefore will I love thee, O amiable Redeemer! who hast loved me even unto death, and hast left me in this Sacrament, the sweetest pledge of thy affection. Oh! inflame my heart, burn and consume it with this heavenly fire; let me love thee above all things; let me love thee, more than myself; let me adhere to thee always; let me never be separated from thee. Yes, my God! I love thee with all my heart, with all my strength. I love thee for thy own sake, and I heartily wish that every object on earth may increase my love for thee. If I cannot love thee, as much as I desire, as much as thou hast loved me, as much as thou deservest to be loved may I at least, love thee as much as I am able. Let disgust and anguish embitter every other attachment, that I may be happily forced to rest in thee alone. Make this love, I beseech thee, effectual, ardent and persevering, that its divine influence may support me in every trial, may purify my affections, and bring me securely to thee.

AN ACT OF OBLATION

O FATHER of mercies, and God of all consolation, how hast thou loved us, to whom thou hast given thy only begotten Son, once for our ransom, and daily for the food of our souls! What can I, a wretched creature, return thee for this infinite charity! Verily nothing else but this same beloved Son of thine, whom thou hast given me, and surely thou couldst give me nothing greater, or more worthy of thyself. Him then I offer to thee, O heavenly Father, with whom thou art always well pleased; him, whom thou hast lovingly delivered up to death for me, and given me in this most holy sacrament, which we frequent for the everlasting memorial of his death.. He is our High Priest and Victim; he is the Propitiation for the sins of the whole world; he is our Advocate and Intercessor. Look down then upon him, and for his sake look down upon me, and upon us all. Remember all his sufferings, which he endured here in his mortal life, his bitter anguish, his mortal agony and bloody sweat, all the injuries and affronts, all the blows and stripes, all the bruises and wounds that he received for us. Remember his death, which thou wast pleased should be the fountain of our life; and for the sake of his sacred passion, have mercy on us. Receive, O holy Father, Almighty and Eternal God! this holy and unspotted Victim, which I here offer thee, in union with that love, with which he offered himself to thee upon the altar of the cross. Receive him for the praise and glory of thy name; in thanksgiving for all the benefits bestowed on me, and on all mankind; in satisfaction also for all my sins, and for the benefit of thy whole Church, and the refreshment and succor of all thy faithful, living and dead, through the same Lord Jesus Christ thy Son.

AN ACT OF THANKSGIVING

When I reflect, O my God! on the innumerable blessings and favors thou hast heaped on me, from the first moment of my existence to the present hour, I am penetrated with confusion; and my heart, overpowered with gratitude and love, is unable to express what I feel. I am surrounded on all sides with thy benefits. Thou art not only the God of the universe; thou art also, in a special manner, a God to me; so interested art thou in all that concerns my welfare, that thy attention seems to be fixed on me alone. Thou hast given me all that I am, and even all that thou art thyself. I can call thee, with as much reason as David could, *the God of my salvation, and my mercy*; my refuge and my support; my treasure and my inheritance.

What do I say? Dost thou not deign at present to become my nourishment, to incorporate thyself with my very substance, that I may know the extent of thy love, and possess within my breast a pledge of eternal life? How great, then, will be my ingratitude, if henceforward I do not endeavor, to the utmost of my ability, to correspond with this infinite love, this marked predilection! O my God! may I never be unmindful of thy favors! may my right hand be forgotten, and my tongue cleave to my mouth, if ever I neglect to extol thy mercies! But how shall I, a wretched, miserable creature, make thee a suitable return for all thou hast done for me? In myself I have nothing; but do I not possess, in the invaluable gift I have just received, an adequate thanksgiving? an offering worthy of thy supreme greatness?

Accept then, O omnipotent Lord! the uninterrupted praise and thanksgivings which thy dear Son offered thee from the moment of his incarnation, to the close of his mortal life; particularly at the institution of this sacrament, when fully sensible of our weaknesses, and of the infinite value of the benefits then bestowed, he raised his eyes to thee, O omnipotent Father! and in our name gave thanks. The sacrifice of my whole being is not worthy to be presented to thee; but in offering thee to thyself, I look on my debts as abundantly discharged. May thy infinite mercies be for ever exalted, for having given me so excellent a means of repaying, in some manner, all the obligations I have contracted towards thy justice, as well as thy mercy.

AN ACT OF PETITION

O MOST merciful Saviour! thou seest all my maladies, and all the wounds of my soul; thou knowest how prone I am to evil, and how backward and sluggish to good. Thou seest this self-love, that tyrannizes over my soul, which is so deeply rooted in my corrupt nature, and branches out into so many vices, so much pride and vanity, so much passion and envy, so much covetousness and worldly solicitude, so much sensuality and concupiscence. Oh! who can heal all these my evils, but thou, the true physician of my soul, who givest me thy body and blood in this blessed sacrament, as a sovereign medicine for all my infirmities, and a sovereign balsam for all my wounds. Dispel the darkness of ignorance and error from my understanding, by thy heavenly light drive away the corruption and malice of my will, by the fire of divine love and charity; restrain all the motions of concupiscence, and all the irregular sallies of passion, that they may no more prevail over me; strengthen my weakness with heavenly fortitude; destroy this monster of self-love, with its many heads, or, at least, chain down this worst of all my enemies, that it may no longer usurp the empire of my soul, which belongs to thee, and which thou hast taken possession of, this day; cut off the heads of this beast, and particularly that which annoys me most, and which is my predominant passion; stand by me henceforward in all my temptations, that I may never more be overcome; remove from me all dangerous occasions, and grant me this one favor, that I may rather die a thousand deaths than live to offend thee deliberately.

O my Jesus! thou art infinitely rich, and all the treasuries of divine grace are locked up in thee; these treasures thou bringest with thee, when thou comest to visit us in this blessed sacrament, and thou takest an infinite pleasure in opening them to us, to enrich our poverty. This gives me the confidence to present thee now with my petitions, and to beg of thee those graces and virtues, which I so much need, as thou best knowest. Oh! increase and strengthen my belief of thy heavenly truths. and grant that henceforward I may ever live by faith, and be guided by the maxims of thy Gospel. Teach me to be poor in spirit, to take off my heart from the love of these transitory things, and to fix it upon eternity; teach me, by thy divine example, and by thy most efficacious grace, to be meek and humble of heart, and in my patience to possess my soul. Grant that I may ever keep my body and soul chaste and pure; that I may ever bewail my past sins, and by a daily mortification restrain all irregular inclinations and passions for the future. Above all things, teach me to love thee; teach me to be ever recollected in thee, and to walk always in thy presence; teach me to love my friends in thee, and my enemies for thee; grant me the grace to persevere to the end in this love. Let nothing in future be my comfort, but thou, O Divine Jesus! nor let any thing afflict me hereafter but my sins and whatever is displeasing to thy Divine Majesty. O Soul of Christ, sanctify me; Body of Christ, save me; Blood of Christ, purify me; Water issuing from the side of Christ, wash me; Passion of Christ, strengthen me. O good Jesus, graciously hear me; hide me within thy wounds; suffer me never to be separated from thee; call me at the hour of death, and command me to come to thee, that I may associate with the saints and angels, and the whole choir of celestial spirits, to sing forth canticles of praise and glory to thy holy name for ever and ever, world without end. Amen, amen, sweet Jesus! *Amen.*

A PRAYER OF ST. THOMAS OF AQUINAS

I give thee thanks, eternal Father; for having, out of thy pure mercy, without any deserts of mine, been pleased to feed my soul with the body and blood of thy only son, our Lord Jesus Christ. I beseech thee, that this holy communion may not be to my condemnation, but prove an effectual remission of all my sins. May it strengthen my faith; encourage me in all that is good; deliver me from my vicious customs; remove all concupiscence; perfect me in charity, patience, humility, obedience, and in all other virtues. May it secure me against all the snares of my enemies, both visible and invisible; perfectly moderate all my inclinations, closely, unite me to thee, the true and only good. and happily settle me in unchangeable bliss. I now make it my hearty request, that thou wilt one day admit me, though an unworthy sinner, to be a guest at that divine banquet, where thou, with thy Son and the Holy Ghost, art the true light, eternal fullness, everlasting joy, and perfect happiness of all the saints, through the same Jesus Christ, our Lord. *Amen.*

Devotions to the Blessed Sacrament

Devout Prayers

I

O most adorable Jesus! whom thy own infinite love induces to dwell among us, thy unworthy servants, in the adorable Sacrament of the Altar, receive, I beseech thee, my profound adoration. I firmly believe that thou art really present in the holy Eucharist, as powerful, as amiable, and as adorable as thou art in heaven; thou hast mercifully hidden the splendor of thy Majesty, lest it should deter us from approaching thy sanctuary. I believe thou dwellest on our altars, not only to receive our adorations, but to listen to our petitions, to remedy our evils, to be the strength and nourishment of our souls, our powerful helper, our refuge and our sacrifice. I hope in that boundless mercy which detains thee among us, poor weak sinners. I love that infinite goodness, which induces thee to communicate thyself so liberally and so wonderfully to thy creatures: I thank thee for so convincing a proof of thy love, and ardently Wish that I could worthily acknowledge all the blessings I have ever received from this fountain of grace and mercy. I sincerely regret that this precious pledge of thy love is received by so many with such coldness and indifference.

Alas! I myself have had too much share, by my ungrateful conduct, in wounding thy merciful heart on this altar, and I am more guilty than others, since very few have been so much favored. Thou hast not only granted me abundantly the general blessings, which this fountain of grace pours on the world; but thou hast provided me with the most favorable opportunities of loving and. adoring thee in this august mystery.

Thou hast placed me close to thy sanctuary, where I can recur to thee frequently, and daily behold the sacrifice on the altar. Ah! my good God! I am now convinced that thou deservest from me all the love that my heart is capable of feeling; therefore, I humbly consecrate to thee all my affections, and firmly resolve, from this moment, to endeavor to imitate the respect, gratitude, and love, which always distinguished those among thy faithful servants, who were most peculiarly devoted to the august Sacrament of the Altar. Accept, O Divine Jesus! all the sacrifices of Mass, that have been offered, and that will be offered hereafter, throughout the whole world, in thanksgiving for the institution of this amiable mystery: in atonement for all the insults, irreverences, and sacrileges which have ever been committed against it. and to implore for myself and all creatures a solid devotion to the holy Eucharist. Mercifully give efficacy to my ardent desire of worthily honoring thee in this adorable mystery, and grant me, through thy divine heart, a share in the purity and fervor of the angels, who day and night surround thy sanctuary, and of all those who have loved thee most in this sacred mystery; that I may serve thee with sincerity and perseverance during my life, and be so happy as to enjoy thee in the splendor of thy glory for all eternity. *Amen.*

II

O MY God, my most adorable Refuge! terrified at my own weakness, covered with the wounds I have already received, solicited by innumerable passions to offend thee anew, and tortured by the apprehension of being at this moment an object of thy just indignation, I throw myself at the foot of this altar. O Lord! thou, in whose *sight the stars are not pure*, cast me not away from thy face, and take not thy holy spirit from me. I have , often and grievously offended thee: I know not whether thou hast pardoned me, or whether I am worthy of love or hatred; I am engaged in a conflict, to which, of myself, I am unequal; and by the abuse of the favors thou hast hitherto granted me, I have rendered myself unworthy of those special graces, which are necessary to conquer such enemies as mine. Pursued by unceasing solicitations to offend thee, my sovereign God! wearied by my evil inclinations, and disgusted with the fund of depravity, which lies lurking in my heart, I too often doubt whether I may not have committed the evil which I sovereignly dread; and am even on the point of wounding thy adorable heart, by despairing of that mercy which cannot be exhausted by ingratitude even greater than mine. O my God! all my misery is before thee, and my conflicts arc not hidden from thy sight: thou hast not forbidden thy children to complain to thee, to lay their griefs at thy feet, and pour their sorrows into that paternal bosom, where the good and the weak find a secure refuge. Ah! why have I so long delayed to seek thee, my divine Comforter? why have I not always fled to thee in this most amiable Sacrament, where thou art to all who hope in thee, a Helper, a Deliverer, a Tower of strength from the face of their enemies? Behold me now, my God and Redeemer! behold me at thy sacred feet, oppressed; and pursued by inveterate foes, whom thou alone canst put to flight. Arise, then, adorable Jesus! arise, and judge thy own cause; abandon not a soul which combats in thy name, and for thy love; *be thou unto me a God, a Protector, and* let this august tabernacle be to me *a house of refuge*, where thou, my divine Master, wilt not only preserve me from grievous falls, but also instruct me in that sublime perfection, which springs from humility of heart, and which teaches to detest sin, but at the same time to embrace the abjection which springs therefrom, and dwell with joy on the conviction which it creates of the innate misery of our weak natures. Ah! why should I despond? Am I not resolved to die a thousand deaths rather than offend thee? Yes, my adorable Saviour! I will, with the assistance of thy grace, resist all that is contrary, not only to thy law, but to the perfection of thy love; and all the torments of hell itself I would infinitely prefer to the enjoyment of any worldly delight, which would separate me from thee. For these dispositions, O Lord! I most fervently thank thy boundless mercy; they come not from myself, but are the effects of thy grace, which is with me, notwithstanding my unworthiness.

I will then confidently hope in thy assistance, in that mercy which is above all thy works, and once more cast myself, and all that I am, and have, into thy divine bosom: I commit my salvation to thy care; for I am well convinced that it is dearer to thee, than it can be to me, and that thou wilt never abandon a soul, which thou didst not consider too highly purchased by the sacrifice of thy precious life.

III

O MY God, my adorable Love! I am firmly convinced that the heart made for thee, will be satisfied with nothing less than thyself. I consecrate myself for ever to thee in this august mystery, persuaded that the soul created to feast on thy adorable charms, can never be so happily; so profitably employed, as in contemplating the most wonderful miracle of thy mercy and love. Come then into my heart, that I may enter into thine. Come, and by one sweet transport of thy love, concentrate every power of my soul in thee. Teach me, my heavenly Spouse! to spare no exertion in thy service; to despise, and for ever renounce every gratification which this world can bestow, that I may deserve to repose in thy arms, to lean on thy bosom, with thy beloved disciple, and to taste and see how sweet thou art. Adorable heart of Jesus, delicious abode of the just, and secure refuge of sinners! receive me: *thou art my rest for ever and ever*—in thee *will I dwell, for I have chosen it.*

DEVOUT ASPIRATIONS

O SOUL of Christ, sanctify me. Body of Christ, save me. Blood of Christ, inebriate me. Water of the side of Christ, purify me. Passion of Christ, comfort me. O good Jesus, hear me. Within thy sacred wounds shelter me. Never suffer me to be separated from thee. From the malice of my enemies, defend me. At the hour of my death, call me. Command me to come to thee, that, with thy saints, I may praise thee for over and ever. *Amen.*

OTHER DEVOUT ASPIRATIONS

Blood of Jesus, wash me.

Passion of Jesus, strengthen me.

Wounds of Jesus, heal me.

Heart of Jesus, receive me.

Spirit of Jesus, enliven me.

Love of Jesus, inflame me.

Mercy of Jesus, spare me.

Cross of Jesus, support me.

Thorns of Jesus, crown me.

Sighs of Jesus, plead for me.

Agony of Jesus, atone for me.

Lips of Jesus, bless me in life and death, in time and in eternity. *Amen.*

The Rosary of the Blessed Virgin Mary

In the name of the Father, &c.

I believe in God, &c.

V. Hail Mary, full of grace, the Lord is with thee.

R. Blessed art thou amongst women, and blessed is the fruit of thy womb, Jesus.

V. Thou, O Lord, will open my lips.

R. And my tongue shall announce thy praise.

V. Incline unto my aid, O God:

R. O Lord, make haste to help me. Glory be to the Father, &c.

[*Alleluia*, is said at all times except from Septuagesima till Easter, during which period, say:]

Praise be to thee, O Lord, King of eternal glory.

THE FIVE JOYFUL MYSTERIES

1. *The Incarnation.*

LET us contemplate in this Mystery, how the Angel Gabriel saluted our blessed Lady with the title of Full of Grace, and declared unto her; the Incarnation of our Lord and Saviour Jesus Christ.

Then say, *Our Father*, &c., once, *Hail Mary*, &c., ten times.

When the *Hail Mary* has been repeated a tenth time, the decade finishes with *Glory be to the father*, &c., then follows the prayer.

LET US PRAY

O HOLY Mary, Queen of virgins! by the most high mystery of the Incarnation of thy beloved Son, our Lord Jesus Christ, by which our salvation was so happily begun, obtain for us, by thy intercession, light to know this so great a benefit which he hath bestowed upon us, vouchsafing in it to make himself our brother, and thee, (his own most beloved mother,) our mother also. *Amen.*

II. *The Visitation*

LET us contemplate in this Mystery, how the Blessed Virgin Mary, understanding from the angel, that her cousin St. Elizabeth had conceived, went with haste into the mountains of Judea, to visit her, and remained with her three months. *Our Father, &c.*

LET US PRAY

O HOLY Virgin, most spotless mirror of humility; by that exceeding charity which moved thee to visit thy holy cousin St. Elizabeth, obtain for us, by thy intercession, that our hearts may be so visited by thy most holy Son, that being free from all sin, we may praise him and give him thanks for ever. *Amen.*

III. *The birth of our Lord Jesus Christ, in Bethlehem*

LET us contemplate in this Mystery, how the Blessed Virgin Mary, when the time of her delivery was come, brought forth our Redeemer, Christ Jesus, at midnight, and laid him in a manger, because there was no room for him in the inns at Bethlehem. *Our Father, &c.*

LET US PRAY

O MOST pure Mother of God, by thy virginal and most joyful delivery, in which thou gavest unto the world thy only Son, our Saviour, we beseech thee to obtain for us, by thy intercession, grace to lead so pure and holy lives in this world, that we may worthily sing without ceasing, both day and night, the mercies of thy Son, and his benefits to us by thee. Amen.

IV. *The Oblation of our blessed Lord in the Temple*

LET us contemplate in this Mystery, how the most Blessed Virgin Mary, on the day of her purification, presented the child Jesus in the temple, where holy Simeon, giving thanks to God with great devotion, received him into his arms. *Our Father, &c.*

LET US PRAY

O HOLY Virgin, most admirable mistress and pattern of obedience, who didst present in the temple the Lord of the temple, obtain for us of thy beloved Son, that, with holy Simeon and devout Anna, we may praise and glorify him for ever. *Amen.*

V. *The finding of the child Jesus in the Temple*

LET us contemplate in this Mystery how the Blessed Virgin Mary, having lost without any fault of hers her beloved Son in Jerusalem; she sought him for the space of three days, and at length found him the third day in the temple, in the midst of the doctors, disputing with them, being of the age of twelve years. *Our Father, &c.*

LET US PRAY

MOST Blessed Virgin, more than martyr in thy sufferings, and yet the comfort of such as are afflicted; by that unspeakable joy, wherewith thy soul was ravished in finding thy beloved Son in the temple, in the midst of the doctors, disputing with them, obtain of him for us, so to seek him, and to find him in the holy Catholic Church, that we may never be separated from him. *Amen.*

SALVE REGINA

HAIL, holy Queen, Mother of Mercy, our life, our sweetness, and our hope! to thee we cry, poor banished children of Eve; to thee we send up our sighs, mourning and weeping in this valley of tears. Turn, then, most gracious advocate, thy eyes of mercy towards us, and after this our exile is ended, show unto us the blessed fruit of thy womb, Jesus: O clement, O pious, O sweet Virgin Mary.

V. Pray for us, O holy Mother of God.

R. That we may be made worthy of the promises of Christ.

LET US PRAY

O God, whose only begotten Son, by his life, death and resurrection, has purchased for us the rewards of eternal life; grant, we beseech thee, that meditating upon those mysteries, in the most holy Rosary of the Blessed Virgin Mary, we may imitate what they contain, and obtain what they promise: Through the same Christ our Lord. *Amen.*

THE FIVE DOLOROUS MYSTERIES

I. *The prayer and bloody sweat of our blessed Saviour in the Garden*

LET us contemplate in this Mystery, how our Lord Jesus was so afflicted for us in the garden of Gethsemani, that his body was bathed in a bloody sweat, which ran trickling down in great drops to the ground.

Our Father, &c. Hail Mary, &c. Glory be to the Father, &c., as before.

LET US PRAY

MOST holy Virgin, more than martyr, by that ardent prayer which thy most beloved Son poured forth unto his

Father in the garden, vouchsafe to intercede for us, that our passions being reduced to the obedience of reason, we may always, and in all things, conform and subject ourselves to the will of God. *Amen.*

II. *The scourging of our blessed Lord at the Pillar*

LET us contemplate in this Mystery, how our Lord Jesus Christ was, most cruelly scourged in Pilate's house, the number of stripes they gave him being above five thousand, (as it was revealed to St. Bridget.) *Our Father, &c.*

LET US PRAY

O MOTHER of God, overflowing fountain of patience; by those stripes thy only and most beloved Son vouchsafed to suffer for us, obtain of him for us grace that we may know how to mortify our rebellious senses, and cut off all occasions of sinning, with that sword of grief and compassion, which pierced thy most tender soul. *Amen.*

III. *The crowning of our blessed Saviour with Thorns*

LET us contemplate in this Mystery, how those cruel ministers of Satan platted a crown of sharp thorns, and most cruelly pressed it on the sacred head of our Lord Jesus Christ. *Our Father, &c.*

LET US PRAY

O MOTHER of our eternal Prince and King of glory; by those sharp thorns, wherewith his most holy head was pierced, we beseech thee, that, by thy intercession, we may be delivered here from all motions of pride, and, in the day of judgment, from that confusion which our sins deserve. *Amen.*

IV. *Jesus carrying his Cross*

LET us contemplate in this Mystery, how our Lord Jesus Christ, being sentenced to die, bore with the most amazing patience the cross, which was laid upon him for his greater torment and ignominy. *Our Father, &c.*

LET US PRAY

O HOLY Virgin, example of patience, by the most painful carrying of the cross, in which thy Son, our Lord Jesus Christ, bore the heavy weight of our sins, obtain of him for us, by thy intercession, courage and strength to follow his steps, and bear our cross after him to the end of our lives. *Amen.*

V. *The crucifixion of our Lord Jesus Christ*

LET us contemplate in this Mystery, how our Lord and Saviour Jesus Christ, being come to Mount Calvary, was stript of his clothes, and his hands and feet most cruelly nailed to the cross, in the presence of his most afflicted Mother. *Our Father, &c.*

LET US PRAY

O HOLY Mary, Mother of God, as the body of thy beloved Son was for us extended on the cross, so may our desires be daily more and more stretched out in his service, and our hearts wounded with compassion of his most bitter passion.

And thou, O most B. Virgin, graciously vouchsafe to help us to accomplish the work of our salvation, by thy powerful intercession. Amen.

Hail, holy Queen, &c., with the verse and prayer as before, at page 80.

THE FIVE GLORIOUS MYSTERIES

1. *The resurrection of Christ from the Dead*

LET us contemplate in this Mystery, how our Lord Jesus Christ, triumphing gloriously over death, rose again the third day, immortal and impassible.

Our Father, &c. Hail Mary, &c. Glory be to the Father, &c. as before.

LET US PRAY

O GLORIOUS Virgin Mary, by that unspeakable joy thou receivedst in the resurrection of thy only Son, we beseech thee, obtain of him for us, that our hearts may never go astray after the false joys of this world, but may be ever and wholly employed in the pursuit of the only true and solid joys of heaven. *Amen.*

II. *The ascension of Christ into Heaven*

LET us contemplate in this Mystery, how our Lord Jesus Christ, forty days after his resurrection. ascended into heaven attended by Angels, in the sight of his most holy Mother, his holy Apostles and disciples, to the great admiration of them all. *Our Father, &c.*

LET US PRAY

O MOTHER of God, comfort of the afflicted; as thy beloved Son, when he ascended into heaven, lifted up his hands, and blessed his apostles: so vouchsafe, most holy Mother, to lift up thy pure hands to him for us, that we may enjoy the benefit of his blessing and thine, here on earth, and hereafter in heaven. *Amen.*

III. *The coming of the Holy Ghost to his Disciples*

LET us contemplate in this Mystery how our Lord Jesus Christ, being seated on the right hand of God, sent, as he had promised, the Holy Ghost upon the Apostles, who, after he was ascended, returned to Jerusalem, and continued in prayer and supplication with the blessed Virgin Mary, expecting the performance of his promise. *Our Father, &c.*

LET US PRAY

O SACRED Virgin, tabernacle of the Holy Ghost; we beseech thee, obtain by thy intercession, that this most sweet comforter, whom thy beloved Son sent down upon his Apostles, filling them thereby with a spiritual joy, may teach us, in this world, the true way of salvation, and make us walk in the path of virtue and good works. *Amen.*

IV. *The assumption of the Blessed Virgin Mary into Heaven*

LET us contemplate in this Mystery, how the glorious Virgin Mary, after the resurrection of her Son, passed out of this world unto him, and was by him assumed into heaven, accompanied by-the holy Angels. *Our Father, &c.*

LET US PRAY

O MOST prudent Virgin, who, entering into the heavenly palace, didst fill the holy Angels with joy, and man with hope; vouchsafe to intercede for us in the hour of death, that, free from the illusions and temptations of the devil, we may joyfully and successfully pass out of this temporal state to enjoy the happiness of eternal life. *Amen.*

V. *The coronation of the most Blessed Virgin Mary in Heaven*

LET us contemplate in this Mystery, how the glorious Virgin Mary was, with great jubilee and exultation of the whole court of heaven, and particular glory of all the Saints, crowned by her Son with the brightest diadem of glory. *Our Father, &c.*

LET US PRAY

O GLORIOUS Queen of all the heavenly citizens, we beseech thee, accept this Rosary, which, as a crown of roses, we offer at thy feet; and grant, most gracious Lady, that by thy intercession, our souls may he inflamed with so ardent a desire of seeing thee so gloriously crowned, that it may never die in us, until it shall be changed into the happy fruition of thy blessed sight. *Amen.*

Hail, holy Queen, &c., with the verse and prayer as before, at page 80.

PRAYER OF ST. BERNARD

To the Blessed Virgin Mary

REMEMBER, O most pious Virgin Mary! that no one ever had recourse to thy protection, implored thy help, or sought thy mediation, without obtaining relief. Confiding, then, in thy goodness and mercy, I cast myself at thy sacred feet, and do most humbly supplicate thee, O Mother of the eternal Word! to adopt me as thy child, and take upon thyself the care of my salvation. Oh! let it not be said, my dearest Mother, that I have perished where no one ever found but grace and salvation. *Amen.*

A PRAYER

To Our Angel Guardian

O HOLY Angel! to whose care God in his mercy hath committed me; thou, who assistest me in my wants, who consolest me in my afflictions, who supportest me when dejected, and who constantly obtainest for me new favors; I return thee now most sincere and humble thanks, and I conjure thee, O amiable Guide! to continue still thy care; to defend me against my enemies; to remove from me the occasions of sin; to obtain for me a docility to thy holy inspirations; to protect me, in particular, at the hour of my death; and then conduct me to the mansions of eternal repose. *Amen.*

The Litany of Saints

Lord, have mercy on us.
Christ, have mercy on us.
Lord, have mercy on us.
Christ, hear us: Christ, graciously hear us.
God the Father of Heaven, *have mercy on us.*
God the Son, Redeemer of the world, *Have mercy on us.*
God the Holy Ghost, *Have mercy on us.*
Holy Trinity, one God, *Have mercy on us.*
Holy Mary, *Pray for us.*
Holy Mother of God,
Holy Virgin of Virgins,
St. Michael,
St. Gabriel,
St. Raphael,
All ye holy Angels and Archangels,
All ye holy orders of blessed Spirits,
St. John the Baptist,
St. Joseph,
All ye holy Patriarchs and Prophets,
St. Peter,
St. Paul,
St. Andrew,
St. James, (*Son of Zeb.*)
St. John,
St. Thomas,
St. James, (*Son of Alph.*)
St. Philip,
St. Bartholomew,
St. Matthew,
St. Simon,
St. Thaddeus,
St. Matthias,
St. Barnaby,
St. Luke,
St. Mark,

All ye holy Apostles and Evangelists,
All ye holy disciples of our Lord,
All ye holy innocents,
St. Stephen,
St. Laurence,
St. Vincent,
St. Fabian and St. Sebastian,
St. John and St. Paul,
St. Cosmas and St. Damian,
St. Gervase and St. Protase,
All ye holy Martyrs,
St. Sylvester,
St. Gregory,
St. Ambrose,
St. Augustine,
St. Jerome,
St. Martin,
St. Nicholas,
All ye holy Bishops and Confessors,
All ye holy Doctors,
St. Anthony,
St. Bennet,
St. Bernard,
St. Dominick,
St. Francis,
All ye holy Priests and Levites,
All ye holy Monks and Hermits,
St. Mary Magdalen,
St. Agatha,
St. Lucy,
St. Agnes,
St. Cecily,
St. Catharine,
St. Anastasia,
All ye holy Virgins, and Widows;
All ye Men and Women, Saints of God, *make intercession for us.*
Be merciful unto us, *Spare us, O Lord,.*
Be merciful unto us, *Graciously hear us, O Lord.*
From all evil, O Lord *Deliver us.*

From all sin,
From thy wrath,
From a sudden and unprovided death,
From the deceits of the devil,
From anger, hatred,
From the spirit of fornication,
From lightning and tempest,
From everlasting death,
Through the mystery of thy holy incarnation,
Through thy coming,
Through thy nativity,
Through thy baptism and holy fasting,
Through thy cross and passion,
Through thy death and burial,
Through thy holy resurrection,
Through thy admirable ascension,
Through the coming of the Holy Ghost the Comforter,
In the day of judgment,
We sinners, *do beseech thee to hear us.*
That thou spare us, *we beseech thee to hear us.*
That thou pardon us,
That thou vouchsafe to bring to true penance,
That thou vouchsafe to govern and preserve thy holy Church,
That thou vouchsafe to preserve our Apostolic Prelate, and all ecclesiastical orders in thy holy religion,
That thou vouchsafe to humble the enemies of thy holy Church,
That thou vouchsafe to give peace, and true concord to christian kings and princes,
That thou vouchsafe to grant peace, and unity to all christian people,
That thou vouchsafe to confirm and preserve us in thy holy service,
That thou lift up our minds to heavenly desires,
That thou render eternal good things to all our benefactors,
That thou deliver our souls, and those of our brethren, kinsfolks, and benefactors, from eternal damnation,
That thou vouchsafe to give, and preserve the fruits of the

earth,
That thou vouchsafe to give eternal rest to all the faithful departed,
That thou vouchsafe graciously to hear us,
Son of God,
Lamb of God, who takest away the sins of the world, *Spare us, O Lord.*
Lamb of God, who takest away the sins of the world. *Hear us, O Lord.*
Lamb of God, who takest away the sins of the world, *Have mercy on us.*
Christ hear us. *Christ graciously hear us.*
Lord, have mercy on us. *Christ have mercy, on us.*
Lord, have mercy on us. *Our Father, &c.*
V. And lead us not into temptation.
R. But deliver us from evil. Amen.

Psalm 64

O God, come to my assistance; O Lord make haste to help me. Let them be confounded and ashamed that seek my soul:

Let them be turned backward, and blush for shame that desire evils to me:

Let them be presently turned away blushing for shame, that say to me: 'Tis well, 'tis well.

Let all that seek thee, rejoice and be glad in thee; and let such as love thy salvation say always: The Lord be magnified.

But I am needy and poor; O God, help me.

Thou art my helper and my deliverer: O Lord, make no delay.

Glory be to the Father; &c.

V. Save thy servants.

R. Trusting in thee, O my God.

V. Be unto us, O Lord, a tower of strength.

R. From the face of the enemy.

V. Let not the enemy prevail against us at all.

R. Nor the son of iniquity have any power to hurt us.

V. O Lord, deal not with us according to our sins.

R. Neither reward us according to our iniquities.

V. Let us pray for our chief bishop, *N.*

R. The Lord preserve him, and give him life, and make him blessed upon earth, and deliver him not to the will of his enemies.

V. Let us pray for our benefactors.

R. Vouchsafe, O Lord, for thy name's sake, to reward with eternal life all those who have done us good.

V. Let us pray for the faithful departed.

R. Eternal rest give them, O Lord; and let perpetual light shine upon them.

V. May they rest in peace.

R. Amen.

V. For our absent brethren.

R. O my God, save thy servants trusting in thee.

V. Send them help, O Lord, from thy holy place.

R. And from Sion protect them.

V. O Lord, hear my prayer.

R. And let my cry come unto thee.

LET US PRAY

O GOD, whose property is always to have mercy and to spare, receive our petition, that we, and all thy servants who are bound by the chains of sin, may, by the compassion of thy goodness, be mercifully absolved.

Hear, we beseech thee, O Lord, the prayers of thy suppliants, and pardon the sins of them that confess to thee that, in thy bounty, thou mayest give us pardon and peace.

Out of thy clemency, O Lord, show thy unspeakable mercy to us; that so thou mayest both acquit us of our sins, and deliver us from the punishments we deserve for them.

O God, who by sin art offended, and by penance pacified, mercifully regard the prayers of thy people making supplication to thee: and turn away the scourges of thy anger, which we deserve for our sins.

O Almighty and Eternal God, have mercy on thy servant, *N*. our chief bishop, and direct him according to thy clemency, into the way of everlasting salvation; that, by thy grace, he may desire those things that are agreeable to thee, and perform them with all his strength.

O God, from whom art all holy desires, right counsels, and just works, give to thy servants that peace which the world cannot give; that our hearts may be disposed to keep thy commandments, and the fear of enemies being removed, the times, by thy protection, may be peaceable.

Inflame, O Lord, our minds and hearts with the fire of thy holy spirit, that we may serve thee with chaste bodies, and please thee with clean hearts.

O God, the Creator and Redeemer of all the faithful, give to the souls of thy servants departed, the remission of all their sins; that through pious supplications, they may obtain the pardon which they have always desired.

Prevent, we beseech thee, O Lord, our actions by thy holy inspirations, and carry them on by thy gracious assistance; that every prayer and work of ours may begin always from thee, and by thee be happily ended.

O Almighty and Eternal God, who hast dominion over the living and the dead, and art merciful to all whom thou fore-knowest shall be thine by faith and good works; we humbly beseech thee, that they for whom we have determined to offer up our prayers, whether this world still detains them in the flesh, or the world to come has already received them out of their bodies, may, by the clemency of thy goodness, all thy Saints interceding for them, obtain pardon and full remission of all their sins; Through our Lord Jesus Christ, thy son, who liveth and reigneth, one God with thee and the Holy Ghost, world without end. *Amen.*

V. O Lord, hear my prayer.

R. And let my cry come unto thee.

V. May the Almighty and most merciful Lord graciously hear us. R. Amen.

V. And may the souls of the faithful departed, through the mercy of God, rest in peace.

R. Amen!

THE SEVEN

𝔓enitential 𝔓salms

ANTHEM

[Remember not, O Lord! our offenses nor those of our parents, and take not revenge on our sins.]

Psalm 6. *Domine ne, in furore*

LORD, rebuke me not in thy fury; nor chastise me in thy wrath.

Have mercy on me Lord, because I am weak: heal me Lord, because all my bones be troubled.

And my soul is troubled exceedingly: but thou Lord how long?

Turn thee O Lord, and deliver my soul: save me for thy mercy.

Because there is not in death, that is mindful of thee: and in hell who shall confess to thee?

I have labored in my sighing, I will every night wash my bed; I will water my couch with my tears.

My eye is troubled for fury: I have waxen old among all Mine enemies.

Depart from me all ye that work iniquity: because our Lord hath heard the voice of my weeping.

Our Lord hath heard my petition, our Lord hath received my prayer.

Let all Mine enemies be ashamed, & very sore troubled: let them be converted and ashamed very quickly.

Glory be to the Father, and to the Son, and to the Holy Ghost. As it was in the beginning, is now, and ever shalt be, world without end. *Amen.*

Psalm 31. *Beati Quorum*

BLESSED are they, whose iniquities are forgiven: and whose sins be covered.

Blessed is the man, to whom our Lord hath not imputed sin, neither is there guile in his spirit.

Because I held my peace, my bones are inveterated, whiles I cried all the day.

Because day and night thy hand is made heavy upon me: I am turned in my anguish, whiles the thorn is fastened.

I have made my sin known to thee: and my injustice I have not hid.

I said: I will confess against me my injustice to our Lord: and thou hast forgiven the impiety of my sin.

For this shall every holy one pray to thee, in time convenient. But yet in the flood of many waters, they shall not approach to him.

Thou art my refuge from tribulation, which hath compassed me: my exultation, deliver me from them that compass me.

I will give thee understanding, and will instruct thee in the way, that thou shalt go; I will fasten mine eyes upon thee.

Do not become as horse and mule, which have no understanding.

In bit and bridle bind fast their cheeks, that approach not to thee.

Many are the scourges of a sinner, but him that hopeth in our Lord mercy shall compass.

Be joyful in our Lord and rejoice ye just, and Glory all ye right of heart. Glory, &c.

Psalm 37. *Domine, ne in furore.*

LORD rebuke me not in thy fury: nor chastise me in thy wrath.

Because thy arrows are fast sticked in me: and thou hast fastened thy hand upon me.

There is no health in my flesh, at the face of thy wrath: my bones have no peace at the face of my sins.

Because mine iniquities are gone over my head: and as a heavy burden are become heavy upon me.

My scars are putrified and corrupted, because of my foolishness.

I am become miserable, and am made crooked even to the end: I went sorrowful all the day.

Because my loins are filled with illusions: and there is no health in my flesh.

I am afflicted and am humbled exceedingly: I roared for the groaning of my heart.

Lord, before thee is all my desire: and my groaning is not hid from thee.

My heart is troubled, my strength hath forsaken me: and the light of mine eyes, and the same is not with me.

My friends, and my neighbors have approached, & stood against me.

And they that were near me, stood far of: and they did violence which sought my soul.

And they that sought me evils, spake vanities: and meditated guiles all the day.

But I as one deaf did not hear: and as one dumb not opening his mouth.

And I became as a man not hearing: and not having reproofs in his mouth.

Because in thee O Lord have I hoped, thou wilt hear me O Lord my God.

Because I said: Lest sometime mine enemies rejoice over me: and whiles my feet are moved, they speak great things upon me.

Because I am ready for scourges: and my sorrow is in my sight always:

Because I will declare my iniquity: and I will think for my sin.

But mine enemies live, and are confirmed over me: and they are multiplied that hate me unjustly.

They that repay evil things for good, detracted from me: because I followed Goodness.

Forsake me not O Lord my God, depart not from me. Attend unto my help, O Lord the God of my salvation. Glory, &c.

Psalm 50. *Miserere*

HAVE mercy on me O God, according to thy great mercy.

And according to the multitude of thy commiserations, take away Mine iniquity.

Wash me more amply from mine iniquity: & cleanse me from my sin.

Because I do know Mine iniquity: and my sin is before me always.

To thee only have I sinned, and have done evil before thee: that thou mayest be justified in thy words, and mayest overcome when thou art judged.

For behold I was conceived in iniquities: & my mother conceived me in sins.

For behold thou hast loved truth: the uncertain, and hidden things of thy wisdom thou hast made manifest to me.

Thou shalt sprinkle me with hyssop, and I shall be cleansed: thou shalt wash me, and I shall be made whiter then snow.

To my hearing thou shalt give joy and gladness, and the bones humbled shall rejoice. Glory, &c.

Psalm 11 *Domine Exaudi*

LORD hear my prayer: and let my cry come to thee.

Turn not away thy face from me: in what day soever I am in tribulation, incline thine ear to me. In what day soever I shall invocate thee, hear me speedily.

Because my days have vanished as smoke: and my bones are withered as a dry burnt firebrand.

I am striken as grass, and my heart is withered: because I have forgotten to eat my bread.

For the voice of my groaning, my bone hath cleaved to my flesh.

I am become like a pelican of the wilderness: I am become as a night crow in the house.

I have watched, and am become as a sparrow solitary in the housetop.

All the day did mine enemies upbraid me: and they that praised me, sware against me.

Because I did eat ashes as bread, & mingled my drink with weeping.

At the face of thy wrath and indignation: because lifting me up thou hast thrown me down.

My days have declined as a shadow: and I am withered as grass.

But thou O Lord endurest forever: and thy memorial in generation and generation.

Thou rising up shall have mercy on Sion: because it is time to have mercy on it, because the time cometh.

Because the stones thereof have pleased thy servants: and they shall have pity on the earth thereof.

And the Gentiles shall fear thy name O Lord, and all the Kings of the earth thy Glory.

Because our Lord hath built Sion: and he shall be seen in his Glory.

He hath had respect to the prayer of the humble: and he hath not despised their petition.

Let these things be written unto another generation: and the people, that shall be created, shall praise our Lord.

Because he hath looked forth from his high holy place: our Lord from heaven hath looked upon the earth.

That he might hear the groanings of the fettered: that he might loose the children of them that are slain:

That they may show forth the name of our Lord in Sion: and his praise in Jerusalem.

In the assembling of the people together in one, and Kings to serve our Lord.

He answered him in the way of his strength: Show me the fewness of my days.

Call me not back in the half of my days: thy years are unto generation and generation.

In the beginning O Lord thou didst found the earth: and the heavens are the works of thy hands.

They shall perish, but thou art permanent: and they shall all wax old as a garment.

And as a vesture thou shalt change them, and they shall be changed:

but thou art the selfsame, and thy years shall not fail.

The children of thy servants shall inhabit: and their seed shall be directed forever. Glory, &c.

Psalm 129. *De profundis.*

FROM the depths I have cried to thee O Lord: Lord hear my voice:

Let thine ears be intent, to the voice of my petition.

If thou shalt observe iniquities O Lord: Lord who shall sustain it:

Because with thee there is propitiation: and for thy law I have expected thee O Lord.

My soul hath expected in his word: my soul hath hoped in our Lord.

From the morning watch even until night: let Israel hope in our Lord.

Because with our Lord there is mercy: and with him plenteous redemption.

And he shall redeem Israel, from all his iniquities. Glory, &c.

Psalm 142. *Domine exaudi*

LORD hear my prayer: with thine ears receive my petition in thy truth: hear me in thy justice.

And enter not into judgment with thy servant: because no man living shall be justified in thy sight.

Because the enemy hath persecuted my soul: he hath humbled my life in the earth,

He hath set me in obscure places as the dead of the world: and my spirit is in anguish upon me, within me my heart is troubled.

I was mindful of old days, I have meditated in all thy works: in the facts of thy hands did I meditate.

I have stretched forth my hands to thee: my soul is as earth without water unto thee.

Hear me quickly O Lord: my spirit hath fainted.

Turn not away thy face from me: and I shall be like to them that descend into the lake.

Make me hear thy mercy in the morning: because I have hoped in thee.

Make the way known to me, wherein I may walk: because I have lifted up my soul to thee.

Deliver me from mine enemies O Lord, to thee I have fled: teach me to do thy will, because thou art my God.

Thy good spirit will conduct me into the right way: for thy name sake O Lord thou wilt quicken me, in thine equity.

Thou wilt bring forth my soul out of tribulation: and in thy mercy thou wilt destroy mine enemies.

And thou wilt destroy all, that afflict my soul: because I am thy servant. Glory, &c.

Various Prayers

Under Temptations

LORD! thy enemies and mine have risen up against me; they seek my soul to destroy it, and use their utmost efforts to drag it into the bottomless pit: I therefore come, and cast myself at thy feet, to implore thy succor.

Ah! suffer not that soul which thou hast redeemed at the price of thy blood, to become their prey. Be thou my protector and my refuge; receive me into thy arms, and shield me from their rage confound their devices; destroy their power; disappoint their malice. Thy glory, O my Saviour! is concerned in not suffering those that belong to thee, to fall into the hands of thy enemies. Support me, therefore, I beseech thee, in the severe conflicts I have to sustain against them, and make me victorious over all their efforts. *Amen.*

IN SICKNESS.

O MY God! I offer thee the pains which I endure, in expiation of my sins. Alas! I have so often, so grievously, so contemptuously offended thee, who art so full of goodness for me, O my Jesus! who for the love of me didst suffer upon the cross the most excruciating tortures. Alas I what are my sufferings compared with thine? what are they compared with my sins! what are they, compared with the everlasting flames of hell which I have deserved by my horrid crimes! O my God, O sweet Jesus, grant me the grace I stand in need of, to profit by my sufferings, now; to die in thy divine love; and to be happy with thee for ever. Amen.

PRAYERS

For the Ecclesiastical and Civil Authorities.

WE pray thee, O Almighty and Eternal God! who, through Jesus Christ, hast revealed thy glory to all nations, to preserve the works of thy mercy; that thy church, being spread throughout the world, may continue, with unchanging faith, in the confession of thy name.

We pray thee, who alone art good and holy, to endow with heavenly knowledge, sincere zeal, and sanctity of life, our chief bishop *N. N.* the vicar of our Lord Jesus Christ, in the government of his church; our own bishop *N. N.* (*or, if he be not consecrated,*" our bishop elect;") all other bishops, prelates, and pastors of the church; and especially those who are appointed to exercise among us the functions of the holy ministry, and conduct thy people into the ways of salvation.

We pray thee, O God of might, wisdom, and justice! through whom authority is rightly administered, laws are enacted, and judgment decreed, assist with thy Holy Spirit of counsel and fortitude, **the PRESIDENT of these CONFEDERATE STATES**; that his administration may be conducted in righteousness, and be eminently useful to thy people, over whom he presides; by encouraging due respect for virtue and religion; by a faithful execution of the laws in justice and mercy, and by restraining vice and immorality. Let the light of thy divine wisdom direct the deliberations of Congress, and shine forth in all their proceedings and laws, framed for our rule and government; so that they may tend to the preservation of peace, the promotion of national happiness, the increase of industry, sobriety, and useful knowledge; and may perpetuate to us the blessings of equal liberty.

We pray for his Excellency the Governor of this State, for the Members of Assembly, for all Judges, Magistrates, and other officers, who are appointed to guard our political welfare; that they may be enabled, by thy powerful protection, to discharge the duties of their respective stations with honesty and ability.

We recommend, likewise, to thy un bounded mercy, all our brethren and fellow-citizens, throughout **THE CONFEDERATE STATES**, that they may be blessed in the knowledge, and sanctified in the observance, of thy most holy law: that they may be preserved in union, and in that peace which the world cannot give; and after enjoying the blessings of this life, be admitted to those which are eternal.

Finally, we pray thee, O Lord of mercy! to remember the souls of thy servants departed, who are gone before us, with, the sign of faith, and repose in the sleep of peace; the souls of our parents, relations, and friends; of those, who, when living, were members of this congregation, and particularly of such as are lately deceased; of all benefactors, who by their donations or legacies to this church, witnessed their zeal for the decency of divine worship, and proved their claim to our grateful and charitable remembrance. To these, O Lord, and to all that rest in Christ, grant we beseech thee, a place of refreshment, light, and everlasting peace, through the same Jesus Christ, our Lord and Saviour. *Amen.*

PRAYER FOR ONE'S CONFESSOR.

HEAR, O adorable Saviour! my humble prayer in behalf of him whom thou hath appointed to be my spiritual guide through the difficulties that beset my path. As I desire to hear in his voice the expression of thy holy will in my regard, enlighten him with thy holy inspiration; make him a worthy minister of thy altar, a priest according to thy heart; that his advice may urge me to the performance of the duties incumbent on me as thy child, and finally lead me to everlasting happiness. Give him that peace which the world cannot give; bestow on him an ardent love for thee, and a tender confidence in thy virgin Mother. Grant that he may faithfully discharge all the duties of his exalted station; and be thou, O amiable Jesus! his exceeding great reward during all eternity. I ask these favors of thee for him, through the powerful intercession of Mary, thy spotless and ever blessed Mother. *Amen.*

PRAYER FOR THE SOULS IN PURGATORY

O GOD, whose goodness and mercy are unbounded, listen to the prayers we offer thee in behalf of our suffering brethren in Purgatory. O bountiful Jesus, who upon the cross didst shed the last drop of thy blood for the redemption of mankind, look with compassion upon the sufferings of these dear souls. Let some drops of that precious blood flow upon them, and purify their least stains, and extinguish the devouring flames in which they are plunged. Deliver them, O merciful Jesus, from that place of darkness and tortures, and receive them immediately into thy paternal bosom, there to behold, and praise, and love thee for all eternity. *Amen.*

A PRAYER

*For the conversion of sinners, and of those
separated from the Church.*

Almighty and most merciful Father, who holdest in thy hands the destinies of thy creatures, and who desirest not the death of the sinner, but rather that he be converted and live, hearken to the humble petition which I offer to thee in behalf of those who are separated from thee by a sinful life, or remain out of thy Church which thou has commanded all to obey under pain of incurring thy displeasure. Grant that all may forsake their evil ways, and serve thee faithfully to the end. Enlighten those who belong not to thy fold: open their eyes to a knowledge of thy truth, and give them grace and courage to embrace it. Grant them patience under the sufferings they may have to endure for thy sake; and guide them through the thorny path of this world to the endless happiness of the world to come. I ask these favors of thee, O merciful Father! through the merits of thy adorable Son, and through the intercession of his spotless Mother. *Amen.*

Our Father. — Hail Mary.

Instructions and Devotions
for the sick

1. If attacked with serious sickness, send immediately for your confessor, and make a good confession. As sickness is often a punishment of sin, sincere repentance and a good Confession are often means of recovery. Delay not.

2. If your will is not already made, make it, and settle your *temporal affairs*.

3. Ask your best friends candidly to tell you your condition. Admit but few visitors, and profit by the time you have left.

4. Discharge your debts if you have any. Forgive those who have injured you, and ask pardon of all you have injured. Be reconciled to enemies if you have any.

5. With resignation accept your sickness as coming from God, and a just infliction on you for your sins. Offer yourself and your sufferings to God, and beg He will grant you patience. Unite your sufferings with those of Christ our Saviour.

6. Ask some friend to read to you spiritual lessons and prayers.

7. Keep the crucifix before your eyes, and think much and often on the passion and death of our Lord.

8. Try, by frequent acts of contrition, to excite in your soul a truly penitential spirit. It is said by St. Augustine, that however innocent his life may have been no christian ought to venture to die except as a penitent.

A DAILY PRAYER IN TIME OF SICKNESS

LORD Jesus Christ, behold I receive this sickness with which thou art pleased to visit me, as coming from thy fatherly hand. It is thy will it should be thus with me, and therefore I submit: *thy will be done on earth, as it is in heaven.* May this sickness be to the honor of thy holy name, and to the good of my soul. For this end, I here offer myself with an entire submission to thy appointments, to suffer whatever thou pleasest, as long and in what manner thou pleasest. For I thy creature, O Lord, have most ungratefully offended thee; and, as my sins have long since cried aloud to heaven for justice, how can I now complain of thy chastisements? Now, my God, thou are just in all thy ways; I have truly deserved thy punishment; and therefore can have no reason to complain of thee, but rather of my own wickedness.

Rebuke me not, O Lord, in thy fury, nor chastise me in thy wrath; but have compassion on my weakness. Thou knowest my frailty, and that I am nothing but dust and ashes. Deal not with me, therefore, according to my sins, nor punish me according to my iniquities, but according to the multitude of thy tender mercies have compassion on me. May thy justice, O Lord, be tempered with mercy; and let thy heavenly grace come to my assistance, to support me under this illness. Enable me, with strength from above, to bear all the uneasiness, pains, and difficulties of my sickness, with Christian patience, and to accept them with cheerfulness, in just punishment of my offences. Preserve me from all temptations, and be thou to me a tower of strength against the assaults of the enemy, that in this illness I may no ways offend thee. And should it be my last, I beg of thee so to direct me by thy grace, that I may neither neglect nor be deprived of those helps which thou hast, in thy mercy ordained for the safe conduct of my soul in its passage to eternity; that being perfectly cleansed from my sins, I may believe in thee, hope in thee, love thee above all things; and, through the merits of thy death and passion, be admitted into the company of the blessed, where I may praise thee for ever. *Amen.*

*Acts of the most necessary virtues, to be
made in time of sickness.*

LORD, I accept this sickness from thy hands and resign myself entirely to thy blessed will, whether it be for life or death. Not my will, but thine be done; thy will be done on earth, as it is in heaven.

I offer up to thee, O Lord, all that I now suffer, or may hereafter suffer, to be united to the sufferings of my Redeemer, and sanctified by his passion.

I adore thee, O my God and my all, as my first beginning and last end; and, bowing down all the powers of my soul in thy presence, desire to pay thee the best homage I am able.

I desire to praise thee, O Lord, without ceasing, in sickness as well as in health; and to join my heart and voice with the whole church in heaven and on earth, in blessing thee for ever.

I give thee thanks from the bottom of my heart, for all the mercies and blessings bestowed upon me and thy whole church, through Jesus Christ thy Son; and above all, for his having loved me from all eternity, and redeemed me with his precious blood. O let not that blood be shed for me in vain!

Lord, I believe all those heavenly truths which thou hast revealed, and which thy holy Catholic church believes and teaches; thou art the sovereign truth, who canst neither deceive nor be deceived; and thou hast promised the Spirit of truth to guide thy church into all truth. *I believe in God, the Father Almighty, &c.* In this faith I resolve, through thy grace, both to live and die; O Lord, strengthen and increase my faith.

O my God, all my hopes are centered in thee, from whom I hope for mercy, grace, and salvation, through the passion and death of my blessed Redeemer. In thee, O Lord, have I put my trust; O let me never be confounded.

O sweet Jesus, receive me into thy arms in this day of my distress; hide me within thy wounds; bathe my soul in thy precious blood.

I love thee, O my God, with my whole heart and soul, above all things; at least I desire so to love thee. O come now, and take full possession of my soul, and teach me to love thee for ever.

I desire to be dissolved, and to be with Christ.

When, O Lord, will thy kingdom come? When wilt thou perfectly reign in all hearts? When shall sin be no more?

I desire to embrace every neighbor in the arms of perfect charity, for love of thee. I forgive, from my heart, all that have any ways offended or injured me, and ask pardon of all whom I have any ways offended.

Have mercy on me, O God, according to thy great mercy; and, according to the multitude of thy tender mercies, blot out my iniquities.

O who will give water to my head, and fountains of tears to my eyes, that night and day I may bewail all my sins.

O that I had never offended so good a God! O that I had never sinned! Happy are those souls that have preserved their baptismal innocence.

Lord be merciful to me a sinner; sweet Jesus, Son of the living God, have mercy on me.

1 recommend my soul to God, my Creator, who made me out of nothing; to Jesus Christ, my Saviour, who redeemed me with his blood; to the Holy Ghost, who sanctified me in baptism. Into thy hands, O Lord, I commend my spirit.

I renounce from this moment, and for all eternity, the devil and all his works; and abhor all his suggestions and temptations. Suffer not this mortal enemy of my soul, O Lord, to have any dominion over me, either now or at my last hour. O let thy holy angels defend me from all the powers of darkness.

O holy Mary, mother of God, pray for me, a poor sinner, now and at the hour of my death.. O all ye blessed angels and saints of God, pray for me a poor sinner.

[It may also be proper to read some part of the Meditations on the passion of Christ, the Miserere, or other penitential psalms, devout acts of contrition, &c.; but not too much at a time, lest it might fatigue the sick person.]

A DAILY PREPARATION FOR DEATH

1. MY heart is ready, O God, my heart is ready; not my will, but thine be done.

I resign myself entirely to thee, O Lord, to receive death at the time and in the manner it shall please thee to send it.

2. I most humbly ask pardon for all the sins I have committed against thy sovereign goodness, and repent of them all from the bottom of My heart.

3. I firmly believe whatsoever the holy Catholic Church believes and teaches; and by thy grace I will die in this belief.

4. I hope to possess eternal life, through thy infinite mercy and the merits of my Saviour Jesus Christ.

5. O my God, my sovereign good, I desire to love thee above all things, and to despise this miserable world. I desire to love my neighbor as myself, for the love of thee, and from my heart to forgive all injuries.

6. O my divine Jesus, how great is my desire to receive thy sacred body! O come now unto my soul, at least by a

spiritual communion! O grant that I may worthily receive thee before my death! I desire to unite my communion to all the worthy communions which, shall be made in thy holy church, even to the end of the world.

7. Grant me the grace, O my divine Saviour, perfectly to efface all the sins I have committed by any of my senses, by applying daily to my soul thy blessed merits, the holy unction-of thy precious blood.

8. Holy Virgin, Mother of God, defend me from my enemies in my last hour, and present me to thy divine Son. Glorious St. Michael, prince of the heavenly host; my angel guardian, and blessed patrons, intercede for me, and assist me in this my last and dreadful passage.

9. O my God, I renounce all temptations of the enemy, and in general whatsoever may displease thee. I adore and accept thy divine appointments with regard to my soul, and entirely abandon myself to them as most just and equitable.

10. O Jesus, my divine Redeemer, be to me a Saviour. Save me, O my God, hiding myself with an humble confidence in thy dear wounds. I deliver my soul into thy divine hands; receive it into the bosom of thy divine mercy. *Amen.*

Indulgences briefly Explained

The Treasury of the church, consisting of the merits of our Saviour Jesus Christ, of the merits of the Blessed Virgin Mary and of the other saints, is the source from which we may seek aid to make *satisfaction* to God for our sins, after we have sought pardon for them through repentance and absolution. Of this treasury the Sovereign Pontiff, the successor of St. Peter, holds the keys. In virtue of the Communion of Saints we can be made partakers of this spiritual treasury. The application is made to us by what is termed an indulgence. requiring on our part, that we place ourselves in the state of grace, and comply with the prescribed conditions.

An indulgence is not the remission of sin, it is much less a license to sin, but it is *the remission of the temporal punishment, which remains due to sin*, after the sin has been forgiven by means of the sacrament of penance. The temporal punishment and obligation of satisfaction are not always remitted when sin is forgiven, but most commonly are still to be undergone. We know not what will be the amount of satisfaction God will require, nor whether our penitential works, in the imperfect way we perform them, will amount to much in satisfying for our sins, but the church teaches us we can be aided from the riches of the church, which is the mystic body of Christ of which we are weak members, and hence the great importance for us to avail ourselves of the indulgences offered to us, on the condition of our doing certain pious works, in themselves agreeable to God.

There must be a renouncing of sin, a purpose of amendment and satisfaction, a sincere sorrow for sins committed, and a due performance of the conditions prescribed. This penitential disposition must be found in him who seeks the aid of an indulgence.

The church, at an early period of her existence, drew up certain rules or canons for penitential works, to be performed, for a period of days or years or even for the whole life of the penitent, according to the gravity of his sins. The indulgence remitted so many days or so many years of such canonical penances and of the satisfaction which corresponded with them, and such remission was called a *partial indulgence*. An entire remission was called *plenary*. And though the public penances of those canons are not now performed by penitents, yet the obligation of satisfaction being the same, the granting of partial or plenary indulgences still prevails. When these are granted by the competent ecclesiastical authority, and the faithful comply with the conditions with a proper spirit, they obtain from the mercy of God great spiritual favors, for God has said to Him in whose hands He placed the Keys of the Kingdom. of Heaven: "*Whatsoever thou shalt bind upon earth it shall be bound also in heaven: and whatsoever thou shalt loose on earth, it shall be loosed also in heaven.*" Matt. 16:19.

Manner of saying the Rosary or Beads

On the cross, say: THE APOSTLES CREED.

First large bead: OUR FATHER.

On each of the three small beads: THE HAIL MARY.

On the next large one THE GLORY, &c., Then again OUR FATHER, and thus on each large bead; saying the Hail Mary for each small one of every ten or decade.

The substance of the Meditations and Mysteries.

I. *In the joyful mysteries add to the word*
Jesus in the Hail Mary as follows:

1. Who was MADE MAN for us.

2. Whom thou didst carry in visiting St. Elizabeth.

3. Who was born in a stable for us.

4. Who was presented in the temple for us.

5. Whom thou didst find in the temple.

II. *In the Sorrowful Mysteries, say:*

1. Who sweated blood for us.

2. Who was scourged for us.

3. Who was crowned with thorns for us.

4. Who carried the heavy cross for us.

5. Who was crucified for us.

III. *In the Glorious Mysteries say:*

1. Who arose from the dead.

2. Who ascended into Heaven.

3. Who sent the Holy Ghost.

4. Who assumed thee into Heaven.

5. Who crowned thee in Heaven.

CHAPLET OF THE

Immaculate Conception

INVOCATION TO THE SACRED HEART OF JESUS

ADORABLE JESUS! whose divine Heart is ever ready to compassionate the unhappy, have mercy on us, miserable sinners, and grant us the graces we ask through the immaculate and afflicted Heart of thy holy mother and ours also, to whom thou canst refuse nothing. *Amen.*

On the First Bead.—By thy sacred Virginity and Immaculate Conception, O most pure Virgin, Queen of Angels, obtain that my soul and body may be free from all sin. (300 *days indulgence.*)

On the three following.—Ave Maria.

On the fifth.—By thy sacred Virginity, &c.

On the twelve following. O Mary! conceived without sin, pray for us, who have recourse to thee.

(100 days indulgence each time.)

On the last.—By thy sacred Virginity, &c.

In Conclusion, say. — St. Joseph chaste Spouse of the Immaculate Virgin, pray for us, who have recourse to thee, obtain us the love of Jesus and Mary. Jesus, Mary, Joseph! I give you my heart, my soul and my life.

Jesus, Mary, Joseph! assist me in my last agony!

Jesus, Mary, Joseph! grant that I may expire in peace in your holy company.

(100 days indulgence to each of these Invocations.

CONCLUDE WITH THE PRAYER OF
ST. BERNARD.

Remember, O most pious Virgin Mary, that no one ever had recourse to thy protection, implored thy help, or sought thy mediation, without obtaining relief. — Confiding, therefore, in thy goodness and mercy, I cast myself at thy sacred feet, and do most humbly supplicate thee, O Mother of the Eternal Word, to adopt me as thy child, and to take upon thyself the care of my salvation. 0! let it not be said, my dearest Mother, that I have perished where no one ever found but grace and salvation. *Amen.*

ASSOCIATION FOR THE PROPAGATION OF THE FAITH

To assist by alms and prayers, the Catholic missionaries, who are charged with preaching the Gospel to Foreign nations, is the object of this association. Members contribute *one cent* per week. They are to recite daily, one *Our Father* and one *Hail Mary*, and to add this invocation: "*Saint Francis Xavier pray for us.*" The *Our Father* and *Hail Mary* of the Morning or Evening prayer, may be offered for this purpose.

The association is administered by two central councils, one of which is in Lyons, the other in Paris, France. The reports of subscriptions, &c., appear in the *annals of the* Propagation of the Faith, six numbers of which appear annually. Every *ten members* can receive a copy of each number.

The Sovereign Pontiffs, Pius VII, Leo XII, Pius VIII, Gregory XVI, have, by rescript, warmly recommended this association to the faithful, granting indulgences, which may be applied to the souls in purgatory.

The association was first established in Lyons in the year 1822, on the festival of "the Finding of the Holy Cross, and on this Festival a *plenary indulgence* may be gained by the members. Also on the feast of St. Francis Xavier, the patron of the society, and once a month, on any day selected by the member, who each day of the month says the appointed prayers. To gain the indulgence, the member must be sorry for his sins, make his confession, receive holy communion, visit the church or oratory of the Institution, if it have one, and if not, visit the parish church or chapel, and there offer prayers for the prosperity of the church, and the intention of the pope. The sick and infirm, are dispensed from the visit to the church, if with the advice of their confessor they do their best to comply with the other conditions. The indulgence on these festivals can be obtained either on the day, or within the octaves.

A partial indulgence of *one hundred days* can he gained each time that the member says the prescribed prayers with a contrite heart, or makes a donation to the missions, or performs some other pious or charitable work.

ARCHCONFRATERNITY OF THE SACRED AND IMMACULATE HEART OF MARY TO PRAY FOR THE CONVERSION OF SINNERS

This pious Association was established in Paris, at the church of *Notre Dame des Victoires*, Dec. 16, 1836, by the pastor Rev. M. DeGenettes, and approved by the Pope, on the 24th April, 1838, according the privilege of aggregating similar associations. To pray for the conversion of sinners is its primary object.

The chief requirement is, that each associate, after his name has been registered, should recite every day the *Hail Mary* for the intentions of the Association. Besides which, a short act of oblation of the thoughts, words and actions of the day to God through the Holy and Immaculate heart of the ever Blessed Virgin Mary is recommended, with the following short prayers: "Mary, refuge of sinners, pray for us." "0 Mary, conceived without sin, pray for us who have recourse to thee."

It is further recommended, 1st. To receive communion once a month. 2. To recite the fifteen Mysteries of the Rosary once a week, and offer the Communion and Rosary for the intentions of the Association. 3. To wear either the Medal of the

Immaculate Conception, or that known as "the Miraculous Medal." 4. To say, often the prayer of St. Bernard, the Memorare or "Remember."

The Associates, *complying with the usual conditions*, can gain the following plenary indulgences:

1. On the day of Admission.

2. At the hour of Death.

3. On the Sunday before Septuagesima.

4. On the feast of our Lord's circumcision.

5. On the feasts of the Purification, Annunciation, Assumption, Conception, Seven Dolours, and Nativity of our Blessed Lady.

6. On the festival of the conversion of St. Paul, 25th of January.

7. On that of St. Magdalen, July 22d.

8. On any two days of the month the member may select.

9. On the anniversary of their Baptism.

An indulgence of 500 days can be gained by members who assist at the masses celebrated on Saturdays, in honor of the Holy and Immaculate Heart of Mary, in the church or chapel of the confraternity, and there pray for the conversion of sinners.

On the first Saturday of each month a mass is offered for deceased members in the church of Notre Dame des Victoires, at Paris.

THE HOLY SCAPULAR OF OUR LADY OF MOUNT CARMEL

The word *scapular* is derived from the Latin, and signifies a garment worn over the shoulders. The devotion of the Scapular was instituted towards the middle of the 13th century. St. Simon Stock, one of the superiors of the monks of Mount Cannel, in England, established it in consequence of the singular favor extended to him by the Blessed Virgin, who, appearing to him, presented to him the scapular as the livery of her confraternity, a privilege granted to him and to all the Carmelites, with the declaration that *"Whoever shall be so happy as to die wearing this garment, shall not suffer in the eternal flames of Hell."* A promise of protection, which is not interpreted as assuring to the sinner, who wears the scapular, a preservation from eternal punishment if he persevere and die in his sins, but rather a promise to protect him from dying in sin by procuring him the grace of conversion and repentance. This vision occurred on the 16th of July 1251. Since then Popes, Kings, princes, .and the faithful of every rank have sought the protection of the Blessed Virgin by wearing the scapular as her livery.

The bull of Pope John XXII. issued March 3d, 1322, and called the Sabbatine Bull, represents that the Blessed Virgin appeared to him and promised a still greater favor to the members of this devout confraternity, which is, *their deliverance from purgatory*, (if they have been sent there,) *on the Saturday after, their death*. This bull has received the approbation of several of the Sovereign Pontiffs.

To gain the graces and privileges annexed to the scapular, two things are necessary.

1st. The scapular must be received with the accustomed ceremonies from a priest empowered to give it.

2d. It must be devoutly worn, as a scapular, that is hanging from the shoulders. When it is worn out it may be replaced by another, blessed or not, without a new ceremony.

N. B. The pious reception and devout wearing of the scapular, without any special prayers on account of it, is of inestimable advantage to the christian.

But to gain the privileges of the Sabbatine bull, the following conditions must be complied with.

1st. Chastity to be observed according to the state of life of the member.

2dly. Those who can read should each day recite the little office of the Blessed Virgin.

Those who cannot read, instead of the office, must abstain from the use of flesh meat on *Wednesdays* and *Saturdays*.

N. B. Persons who can read are not free to choose the abstinence on Wednesdays and Saturdays, instead of the office of the Blessed Virgin. But for reasons, they may obtain a commutation from a confessor who has the faculty to grant such commutation.

The scapular must be worn continually, night and day, and especially at the hour of death.

Children may be invested and partake of the Sabbatine privilege without being obliged to any thing before the age of seven years. After obtaining the use of reason, they must comply with the conditions to gain the privileges.

The cloth of the scapular must be woolen and of a dark brown color, the two parts attached by woolen strings for wearing part on the breast and part on the back. The picture, and initials I. H. S., usually put on them, are not necessary.

For sharing in the merits and good works of the confraternity, no particular prayer, fast, or abstinence has been prescribed by the church, but each member is free to offer such as his piety will dictate. Those who recite seven *our Father's*, and seven *Hail Mary's* each day, being members, gain an indulgence of forty days, but these are not the prayers prescribed for the Sabbatine privilege, which, as we have said, is the little office of the Blessed Virgin. The others can only take the place of the office by an authoritative commutation.

No one should be deterred from be coming a member by the idea that they cannot read the office of the Blessed Virgin, or perform the abstinence, because by leading a good life and devoutly wearing the scapular, they can gain most of the advantages of the confraternity.

To the members of the scapular of Mount Carmel are granted a plenary indulgence.

1. On the day of admission, (by Pope Paul, V.)

2. On the feast of our Lady of Mount Carmel, July 16, or during the octave, (Paul V., and Benedict XIV.)

3. On the day in each month when there is a procession in honor of the Blessed Virgin, to 'those who assist at it.

4. At the hour of death, for those who pronounce devoutly the holy name of Jesus, or at least say it in their hearts, (Paul V.)

5. Every time that other confraternities have a plenary indulgence, (Sixtus IV, Clement VII.)

6. On all the festivals of the Blessed Virgin, of the twelve Apostles, and of the canonized, saints of the Carmelite order, (Gregory XVI.)

Those who wear the scapular, may on two days in each week at their option,, gain a plenary indulgence, (Gregory XVI.)

Several *indulgencies* can also be gained by the members, as:

1. Of five years and five quarantaines to members who accompany the blessed sacrament to the sick, (Paul V.)

2. Five years and five quarantaines to those who receive holy communion once a month, and pray for the intentions of the Pope.

3. Three hundred days to those who abstain from meat on Wednesday and Saturday.

4. One hundred days each time the member gives an alms or performs some other corporal or spiritual work of mercy.

5. Forty days, once a day, to those who recite seven *our Father's*, and seven *Hail Mary's*, in honor of the seven joys of the Blessed Virgin, viz: The Annunciation, the Visitation, the Nativity, the Adoration of the three Kings, the finding of Jesus in the Temple, the Resurrection, and the Assumption.

N. B. All these by suffrage can be applied to the souls in Purgatory.

THE LIVING ROSARY

This devotion commenced in the city of Lyons in 1826. It was approved by Pope Gregory, XVI, who annexed to it the following indulgences:

The members, who recite the part assigned to them, may gain a plenary indulgence.

1st. On the first festival after their admission.

2d. On the third Sunday of each month.

3d. On the feasts of Christmas, Epiphany, Circumcision, Easter, Ascension, Corpus Christi, Pentecost, and Trinity Sunday; and on all the festivals of the Blessed Virgin, provided they receive the sacraments of penance and the Eucharist on those days, and offer up some prayers in a church.

4. A partial indulgence of one hundred days each time they recite their part during the week.

Also an indulgence of seven years and seven times forty days each time they recite their part on Sunday's and Festivals.

"The Living Rosary" is the union of fifteen persons into a circle for saying the Rosary. The fifteen rosaries being divided, one to each of the fifteen. Thus each recites one *our Father*, ten Hail Mary's, and one *"Glory be to the Father,"* &c., every day in honor of the mystery assigned.

A number of these circles form a sodality under the direction of a clergyman.

The member to whom the first mystery is allotted recites before his decade the *creed*, the *our Father*, and three *Hail Mary's*, which precede the Rosary, and each member concludes his part with this short prayer.

"May the Divine Heart of Jesus, and "the Immaculate Heart of Mary, be ever "known, loved, and imitated in all places "throughout the world."

N. B. Monthly donations are made by the members, to be employed in meeting the expenses of the sodality, for printing, stationary, &c., or procuring vestments and ornaments for the altar. The donation in this country is six cents per month.

Association of prayers for the conversion of those who, in this country, are not in communion with the church.

By a rescript of the 5th September 1852, our Holy Father, Pope Pius, IX, at the instance of the National Council of Baltimore, approves this association, and accords the following indulgences:

1. To those who recite the following prayer:

"Almighty and Eternal God, who savest all, and wilt have none to perish, have regard to the souls who are led astray by the deceits of the devil, that rejecting all errors, the hearts of those who err may be converted, and may return to the unity of thy truth, through Christ our Lord. Amen." The Pope grants a plenary indulgence on receiving the Easter communion.

Also a plenary indulgence at the hour of death, on confessing their sins with sincere sorrow, and receiving the Holy Eucharist; or if unable to receive communion, on their invoking the Holy name of Jesus with their lips, or at least in their hearts.

3. He grants an indulgence of one hundred days each time they recite the above prayer.

4. Those not able to recite the above prayer, may gain these indulgences by daily saying in its place an *our Father*, a *Hail Mary*, and a *Glory*, with the same intention.

VESPERS,

OR

𝕿𝖍𝖊 𝕰𝖛𝖊𝖓𝖎𝖓𝖌 𝕺𝖋𝖋𝖎𝖈𝖊

FOR SUNDAYS

PATER noster, &c., Ave Maria, &c.

V. DEUS, in adjutórium meum inténde.

R. Dómine, ad adjuvándum me festína.

V. Glória Patri, et Fílio, et Spirítui Sancto.

R. Sicut erat in princípio, et nunc, et semper, et in sæcula sæculórum. Amen. Alleluia. *In Lent*: Laus tibi, Domine, Rex aeterne gloriae.

DIXIT Dóminus. Domino meo.* Magna ópera Dómini. Sede a dextris meis:

Donec ponam inimicos tuos,* scabellum pedum tuorum.

Virgam virttitis tuae emittet Dominus ex Sion,* dominare in med ioinimicerum tuorum.

Tecum principium in die virtutis tuae in spendoribus sanctorum* ex utero ante luciferum genui te.

Juravit Dominus, et non

Our Father, &c. Hail Mary, &c.

V. Incline unto my aid, O God.

R. O Lord! Make haste to help me.

V. Glory be to the Father, and to the Son, and to the Holy Ghost.

R. As it was in the beginning, is now, and ever shall be, world without end. Amen Alleleuia. *In Lent*: Praise be to thee O Lord! king of eternal glory.

The Lord said to my Lord: Sit thou at my right hand:

Until I make thy enemies thy footstool.

The Lord will send forth the sceptre of thy power out of Sion: rule thou in the midst of thy enemies.

With thee is the principality in the lay of thy strength; in the brightness of the saints: from the womb before the day-star I begot thee.

poenitebit eum:* Tu es Sacerdos in aeternum secunbum ordinem Melchisedech.

Dominus a dextris tuis,* confregit in die iroe suae reges.

Judicabit in nationibus, Implebit ruinas:* conquassibit capita in terra multorum.

De torrente in via bibet: * propterea exaltabit caput.

Gloria Patri, &c.

The Lord hath sworn, and he will not repent: Thou art a priest for ever according to the order of Melchisedech.

The Lord at thy right hand, hath broken kings in the day of his wrath.

He shall judge among nations; he shall fill ruins: he shall crush the heads in the land of many.

He shall drink of the torrent in the way; therefore shall he lift up the head.

Glory be to the Father, &c.

Psalm 110

CONFITEOR tibi Domine in tote corde meo:* in concilio justorum, et congregatione.

Magna opera:* exguisita in omnes voluntates ejus.

Confessio et magnificentia opus ejus;* et justitia ejus manet in saeculum saeculi.

Memoriam fecit mirabilium suorum; misericors et miserator Dominus:* escam dedit timentibus se.

Memor erit in saeculum testamenti sui:* virtutem operum suorurn annuntiabit populo suo:

I WILL confess to thee O Lord with all my heart: in the counsel of the just, and the congregation.

The works of our Lord are great: exquisite according to all his wills.

Confession and magnificence his work: and his justice continueth forever and Ever.

He hath made a memory of his marvelous works; a merciful and gracious Lord: he hath given meat to them that fear him.

He will be mindful forever of his testament: the force of his works he will show forth to his people:

Ut det illis haereditatem gentium:* Opera manuum ejus, veritas et judicium.

Fidelia Omnia mandata ejus: confirmata in saeulum saeculi;* facta in veritate et aequitate.

Redemptionem misit populo suo:* mandavit in aeternum testamentum suum.

Sanctum, et terribile nomen ejus:* initium sapientiae timor Domini.

Intellectus bonus Omnibus facientibus eum:* landatio ejus manet in saeculum saeculi.

Gloria Patri, &c.

To give them the inheritance of the gentiles: the works of his hands truth, and judgment.

All his commandments are faithful: confirmed forever and ever, made in truth and equity.

He sent redemption to his people: he commanded his testament forever.

Holy, and terrible is his name: the fear of our Lord is the beginning of Wisdom.

Understanding is good to all that do it: his praise remaineth forever and Ever.

Glory, &c.

Psalm 111

BEATUS vir, qui timet Dominum:* in mandatis ejus volet nimis.

Potens in terra erit semen ejus: generaitio rectorum bemecedicetur.

Gloria et divitiae in domo ejus: et justitia ejus manet in saeculum saeculi.

Exortum est in tenebris lumen rectis:* misericors, et miserator, et justus.

Jucundus homo qui miseratur et commodat, disponet sermones suos in judicio:* quia in aeternum non commovebitur.

In memoria aeterna erit justus:* ab auditione mala non timebit.

Paratum cor ejus sperare in

BLESSED is the man that feareth our Lord: he shall have great delight in his commandments.

His seed shall be mighty in the earth: the generation of the righteous shall be blessed,

Glory, and riches in his house: and his justice abideth forever and Ever.

Light is risen up in darkness to the righteous: he is merciful, and pitiful, and just.

Acceptable is the man, that is merciful and lendeth, that shall dispose his words in judgment: Because he shall not be moved forever.

The just shall be in eternal memory: he shall not fear at the hearing of evil.

His heart is ready to hope in

Domino, confirmatum est cor ejus:* non commovebitur donec despiciat inimicos suos.

our Lord, his heart is confirmed: he shall not be moved till he look over his enemies.

Dispersit, dedit pauperibus: justitia ejus manet in saeculum saaculi,* cornu ejus exaltabitur in gloria.

He distributed, he gave to the poor: his justice remaineth forever and ever his horn shall be exalted in Glory.

Peccator videbit, et irascetur, dentibus suis fremet et tabescet:* desiderium peccatorum peribit.

Gloria Patri, &c.

The sinner shall see, and will be angry, he shall gnash his teeth and pine away: the desire of sinners shall perish.

Glory, &c.

Psalm 112.

LAUDATE pueri Dominum: laudate nomen Domini.

PRAISE our Lord ye children: praise ye the name of our Lord.

Sit nomen Domini benedictum,* ex hoc none, et usque in saeculum:

Be the name of our Lord blessed, from henceforth now and forever.

A solis ortu usque ad occasum,* laudabile nomen Domini.

From the rising of the Sun unto the going down, the name of our Lord is laudable.

Excelsus super omnes gentes Dominus, * et super coelos gloria ejus.

Our Lord is high above all nations, and his Glory above the heavens.

Quis sicut Dominus Deus noster, qui in altis habitat;* et humilia respicit in coelo et in terra?

Who is as the Lord our God, that dwelleth on high, and beholdeth the low things in heaven and in earth?

Suscitans a terra inopem,* et de stercore erigens pauperem:

Raising up the needy from the earth, and lifting up the poor out of the dung:

Ut collocet eum cum principibus, * turn principibus populi sui.

To place him with princes, with the princes of his people.

Qui habitare facit sterilem in domo, matrem filiorum

Who maketh the barren woman to dwell in a house, a

laetantem.

Gloria Patria, &c.

joyful mother of children.

Glory, &c.

Psalm 113

In exitu Israel de AEgypto,* domus the Jacob de populo barbaro.

IN the coming forth of Israel out of Ægypt, of the house of Jacob from the barbarous people.

Facta est Judaea sanctificatio ejus,* Israel potestas ejus.

Jewry was made his sanctification, Israel his dominion.

Mare vidit, et fugit:* Jordanis conversus est retrorsum.

The sea saw, and fled: Jordan was turned backward.

Montes exultaverunt ut arietes:* et colles sicut agni ovium?

The mountains leaped as rams: and the little hills as the lambs of sheep.

Quid est tibi mare guod fugisti: et tu Jordanis quia conversis et retrorsum

What aileth thee o sea that thou didst flee: and thou o Jordan, that thou wast turned backward?

Montes exultastis sicut arietes,* et colles sicut agni ovium?

Ye mountains leaped as rams, and ye little hills as the lambs of sheep.

A facie Domini mota est terra, a facie Dei Jacob.

At the face of our Lord was the earth moved, at the face of the God of Jacob.

Qui convertit petram in stagna aquarum,* et rupem in fontes aquarum.

Who turned the rock into pools of waters, and stony hill into fountains of waters.

Non nobis Domine, non nobis: sed nomini tuo da gloriam.

NOT TO US O Lord, NOT TO US: but to thy name give the Glory.

Super miseriordia, tua et veritate tua; nequando dicant gentes: Ubi est Deus eorum?

For thy mercy, and thy truth: lest at any time the Gentiles say: Where is their God?

Deus autem noster in coelo omnia quaecumque voluit, fecit.

But our God is in heaven: he hath done all things whatsoever he would.

Simulacra gentium argentum etaurum,* opera mannum hominum.

Os habent, et non loquentur:* oculos habent, et non videbunt.

Aures habent, et non audient; nares habent, et non odorabunt.

Manus habent, et non palpabunt: pedes habent, et non ambulabunt:* non clamabunt in gutture suo.

Similes illis fiant qui faciunt ea:* et omnes qui confidunt in eis.

Domus Israel speravit in Domino:* adjutor eorum et protector eorrum est.

Domus Aaron speravit in Domino:* adjutor eorum et protector eorum est.

Qui timent Dominum, speraverunt in Domino adjutor eorum et protector eorum est.

Dominus memor fuit nostri;* et benedixit nobis.

Benedixit domui Israel:* benedixit domui Aaron.

Benedixit omnibus, qui timent Dominum,* pusillis cum majoribus.

Adjiciat Dominus super vos;* super vos, et super filios vestros.

Benedicti vos Domino qui fecit coelum et terrain.

Coelum coeli Domino;* terram autem dedit filiis hominum.

Non mortui laudabunt te

The idols of the gentiles are silver, and gold, the works of mens hands.

They have a mouth, and shall not speak: they have eyes, and shall not see.

They have ears, and shall not hear: they have nostrils and shall not smell.

They have hands, and shall not handle: they have feet, and shall not walk: they shall not cry in their throat.

Let them that make them become like to them: and all that have confidence in them.

The house of Israel hath hoped in our Lord: he is their helper and their protector.

The house of Aaron hath hoped in our Lord: he is their helper and their protector.

They that fear our Lord, have hoped in our Lord: he is their helper and their protector.

Our Lord hath been mindful of us: and hath blessed us:

He hath blessed the house of Israel: he hath blessed the house of Aaron.

He hath blessed all, that fear our Lord, the little with the great.

Our Lord add upon you: upon you, & upon your children.

Blessed be you of our Lord, which made heaven, and earth.

The heaven of heaven is to our Lord: but the earth he hath given to the children of men.

Domino: neque omnes, qui descendant in infernum.

Sed nos qui vivimus, benedicimus Domino,* ex hoc nunc et usque in saecularn.

Gloria Patri, &c.

The dead shall not praise thee O Lord: nor all they, that go down to hell.

But we that live, do bless our Lord, from this time, and forever.

Glory, &c.

[The following Psalm is sung on sundry festivals, in place of the foregoing.]

Psalm 116

LAUDATE Dominum omnes gentes:* laudate eum omines populi.

Quioniam confirmata est, super nos misericordia ejus:* et veritas Domini manet in aeternum.

Gloria Patri, &c.

PRAISE our Lord all ye Gentiles: praise him all ye peoples.

Because his mercy is confirmed upon us: and his truth remaineth forever.

Glory, &c.

2 Corinthians 1:2

BENEDICTUS Deus et Pater Domini nostri Jesu Christi, Pater misericordia rum, et Deus totius consolationis, qui consolatur nos in omni tribulatione nostra.

R. Deo gratias.

BLESSED be the God and Father of our Lord Jesus Christ the Father of mercies, and the God of all comfort, who comforteth us in all our tribulation.

R. Thanks be to God.

The Hymn

Lucus Creator optime!
Lucem dierum proferens,

Primordiis lucis novae,
Mundi parans originem.
Qui mane junctum vesperi,
Diem vocari praecipis;
Illabitur tetrum chaos;
Audi preces cum fletibus;
Ne mens, gravata crimine,
Vitae sit exul munere;
Dum nil perenne cogitat,
Seseque culpis illigat.
Coeleste pulset ostium,
Vitale tollat premium
Vitemus omne noxium:
Purgemus omne pessimum.
Praesta, Pater piissime!
Patrique compar unice,
Cum Spiritu Pariclito,
Regnans per omne saeculum.
V. Dirigatur, Domine, oratio mea,
R. Sicut incensum in conspectu tuo.

The Magnificat; or, the Canticle of the blessed Virgin: St. Luke 1

MAGNIFICAT* anima mea Dotminum.

MY SOUL doth magnify our Lord.

Et exultavit Spiritus meus* in Deo salutari meo.

And my spirit hath rejoiced in God my Saviour.

Quia respexit militatem ancillae suae,* ecce enim ex hoc, beatam me dicent omnes generationes.

Because he hath regarded the humility of his handmaid: for behold from henceforth all generations shall call me blessed.

Quia fecit mihi magna qui potens est;* et sanctum nomen ejus.

Because he that is mighty hath done great things unto me, and holy is his name.

Et misericordia ejus a progenie in progenies,* timentibus eum.

Fecit potentiam in brachio suo;* disersit superbos mente cordis sui.

Deposuit, potentes de sede:* et exaltavit humiles.

Esurientes implevit bonis:* et divites dimisit inanes.

Suscepit Israel puerum suum;* recordatus misericordiae suae.

Sicut locutus est ad patres nostros;* Abraham et sernini ejus in saecula.

Gloria Patri, &c.

And his mercy from generation unto generations, to them that fear him.

He hath showed might in his arm: he hath dispersed the proud in the conceit of their heart.

He hath deposed the mighty from their seat, and hath exalted the humble.

The hungry he hath filled with good things: and the rich he hath sent away empty.

He hath received Israel his child, being mindful of his mercy,

As he spake to our fathers, to Abraham and his seed forever.

Glory, &c.

[Then follows the prayer, which is different every Sunday.]

V. Dominus vobiscum.

R. Et cum spiritu tuo.

V. Benedicamus Domino.

R. Deo gritias.

V. Fidelium animas, per misericordiem Dei, requiescant in pace.

R. Amen.

Pater noster, &c.

V. The Lord be with you.

R. And with thy spirit.

V. Let us bless the Lord.

R. Thanks be to God.

V. May the souls of the faithful, through the mercy of God, rest in peace.

R. Amen.

Our Father, &c.

[When Compline is not said immediately after Vespers, after the verse, Fidelium animae, &c. May the souls &c. and Our Father,—is said.

V. Dominus det nobis suam pacem.

R. Et vitam aeternam. Amen.

V. Our Lord grant us his peace!

R. And life everlasting. Amen.

[Then is said one of the following anthems, according to the time.]

The Anthem, from the first Sunday of Advent till the Purification, inclusive.

ALMA Redemptoris mater, quae pervia coeli,

Porta manes, et stella maris, suc curre cadenti,

Surgere qui curat populo, to quae genuisti.

Nature murante, tuum sanctum genitorem,

Virgo prius ac posterius: Gabrielle ab ore,

Sumens illud ave, peccatorum miserere.

MOTHER of Jesus! – heaven's open gate,

Star of the sea, support the fallen state,

Of mortals; thou whose womb thy, maker bore;

And yet, strange thing, a virgin, as before;

Who didst, from Gabriel's hail, this news receive,

Repenting sinners by thy prayers relieve.

In Advent

V. The angel of the Lord declared his message to Mary.

R. And she conceived by the Holy Ghost:

V. Angelus Domini nuntiavit Mariae.

R. Et concepit de Spiritu Sancto.

Oremus

Let us pray

GRATIAM tuam quaesumus Domine! mentibus nostris infunde; ut Angelo nuntiante, Christi, Filii tui incarnationem cognovimus, per passionem ejus et crucem, ad resurrectionis gloriam perducamur, Per

POUR forth, we beseech thee, O Lord! thy grace into our hearts, that we, to whom the incarnation of thy Son has been made known by the message of an angel, may, by his passion and cross, be brought to the

eundem Christum, Dominum nostrum. *R.* Amen.

glory of his resurrection: through the same Christ, our Lord. *R.* Amen

V. Post partum virgo inviolata permansisti.

R. Dei genetrix! intercede pro nobis.

V. After childbirth thou didst remain an inviolate virgin.

R. Mother of God! make intercession for us.

Oremus

Deus! qui salutis aeternae beatee Mariae virgimitate foecunda humano generi praaema praestitisti: tribue, quaesumus, ut ipsam pro nobis intercedere sentiamus, per quam merimus Auctorem vitae suscipere Dominum nostrum Jesum Christum filium tuum. *R.* Amen.

Let us pray

O GOD! who by the fruitful virginity of the blessed virgin Mary, hast given to mankind the rewards of eternal salvation; grant we beseech thee, that we may be sensible of the benefits of her intercession, by whom we have received the Author of life, our Lord Jesus Christ, thy son. *R.* Amen.

From the Purification till Easter

AVE, Regina coelorum!

HAIL, Mary, queen of heavenly spheres!

Ave, Domina angelorum.

Hail, whom the angelic host reveres!

Salve, radix! salve, porta!
Ex qua mundo lux est orta.

Hail, fruitful root, hail sacred gate!

Whence the World's light derives its date.

Gaude, virgo gloriosa!

Super omnes speciosa;

O glorious maid, with beauty blessed!

May joys eternal fill thy breast!

Vale, O v de decora!

Thus crown'd with beauty and with joy.

Et pro nobis Christum exora.

Thy prayers with Christ for

V. Dignare me laudare te, virgosacrata!

R. Da mihi vertutem contra hostes tuos.

V. Vouchsafe, O sacred virgin to accept my praises.

R. Give me power against thy enemies.

Oremus

CONCEDE, misericors Deus fragilitati nostrae praesidium: ut qui sanctae dei genitricis memoriam agimus, intercessionis ejus auxilio a nostris iniquitatibus resurgamus. Per eundem Christum, Dominum nostrum. *R.* Amen.

Let us pray

GRANT us, O mercifal God! strength against all our weakness; that we, who celebrate the memory of the holy mother of God, may, by the help of her intercession, rise again from our iniquities: through the same Christ our Lord. *R.* Amen.

From Easter until Trinity

Regina coeli! laetare, Alleluia:

Quia quem meruisti portare, Alleluia;

Resurrexit, sicut dixit,

Ora pro nobis Deum, Alleluia.

V. Gaude at he, tare, Virgo Maria!

R. Quia surrexit Dominus vere; Alleluia.

O QUEEN of heaven! rejoice, Alleluia;

For he whom thou didst deserve to bear, Alleluia:

Is risen again as he said, Alleluia.

Pray for us to God, Alleluia.

V. Rejoice and be glad, O Virgin Mary! Alleluia.

R. Because our Lord is truly risen, Alleluia.

Oremus

Deus! qui per resurrectionem Fili tui, Domini nostri, Jesu Christi, mundum laetificare dignaftis es, praesta quaesumus, ut ejus genitricem virginem Mariam perpetuae capiamus gaudia vitae. Per eundem Christum, Dominum

Let us pray

O GOD! who by the resurrection of thy Son, our Lord, Jesus Christ, hath been pleased to fill the world with joy; grant we beseech thee, that by the virgin Mary, his mother, we may receive the joys of eternal life: through the same

nostrum. *R.* Amen.   Christ, our Lord. *R.* Amen.

From Trinity Sunday until Advent

SALVE, regina, O mother of mater misericordiae! vita, dulcedo, et spes nostra, salve,

Ad te clamamus, exules filii Evae. Ad te suspiramus, gementes et flentes, in hac lacrymarum valle.

Eia ergo advocata nostra, illos tuos misericordes oculos ad nos converte.

Et Jesum benedictum fructum ventris tui nobis post hoc exilium ostende;

O clemens! O pia! O dulcis Virgo Maria.

V. Ora pro nobis, sancta Dei Genitrix!

R. Ut digni efficiamur promissionibus Christi.

HAIL, O Queen, O mother of mercy! hail, our life, our comfort, and our hope!

We, the banished children of Eve, cry out unto thee. To thee we send up our sighs, groaning and weeping in this vale of tears.

Come, then, our advocate, and look upon us with those thy pitying eyes.

And after this, our banishment, show us Jesus, the blessed fruit of thy womb;

O merciful! O pious! O sweet Virgin Mary!

V. Pray for us, O holy mother of God.

R. That we may be made worthy of the promises of Christ.

Oremus

OMNIPOTENS, sempiterne Deus! qui gloriosae Virginis Matris Mariae corpus et animam, ut dignum Filii tui habitaculum effici mereretur, Spiritu Sancto co-operante, praeparasti; da, ut cujus commemoratione laetamur ejus pia intercessione ab instantibus malis, et a morte perpetua liberemur. Per eundem Christum, Dominum nostrum. *R.* Amen.

V. Divinum auxilium

Let us pray

ALMIGHTY and eternal God! who by the cooperation with the Holy Ghost, didst prepare the body and soul of the glorious virgin mother, Mary, that a worthy habitation for thy Son; grant that as with joy we celebrate her memory, so by her pious intercession we may be delivered from present evils and eternal death: through the same Christ, our Lord, R. Amen.

V. May the divine assistance

maneat seni per nobiscum. *R.* Amen.

always remain with us. *R.* Amen.

HYMNS AND ANTHEMS

WHICH MAY BE SUNG AT THE BENEDICTION OF THE BLESSED SACRAMENT

Ch. ADOREMUS in aeternum Sanctissimum Sacramentum.

Solo. Laudate Dominum, Psalm 116, page 133.

The Same in English.

Prostrate in trembling awe, let's all adore

This holy Sacrament for evermore.

O praise the Lord, Psalm 116, page 133.

O SALUTARIS hostia,
Quae coeli pandis ostium!
Bella premunt hostilia,
Da robur, fer auxillium.

Uni trinoque Domino,
Sit sempiterna gloria;
Qui vitam sine termino
Nobis donet in patria.

The same in English

O SAVING host! O heav'nly bread!
That mak'st our souls for ever live,
Against the cruel foes we dread,
Thy heav'nly aid unto us give.

O thou, who feed'st us with thy blood
Good shepherd! praise be to thy name,
Whilst mortals taste the immortal food,
Let heav'nly choirs thy love proclaim.

PANIS angelicas fit pants hominum,
Dat panis coelicus figuris terminum:
O res mirabilis! manducat Dominum
Pauper, servus at humilis.

Te, trina Deitas, unaque poseimus,
Sic nos to visita, sicut te colimus;
Per tuas semitas duc nos quo tendimus,
Ad lucem quam inhabitas.

The same in English.

THE bread of angels, bread of men is made;
The truth and substance now exclude the shade.
O strange, effect of love! the sovereign God
Becomes the poor's, the slave's, the sinner's food!
O Three and One! we humbly thee implore
To manifest thyself, as we adore;
By thy own way instruct us how to move,
To find the abyss of light, in which thou
dwell's above.

AVE, verum corpus! natum
De Maria Virgine,
Vere passum, immolatum,
In crime pro homine.
Cujus latus perforatum
Unda fluxit sanguine,
Esto nobis praegustatum,
Mortis in examine.

O Jesu dulcis!
O Jesu pie!
O Jesu fili Mariae!
Tu nobis miserere.

The same in English.

HAIL! real body of our Lord,
From spotless Virgin born!
Hail! Victim, stretch'd upon the cross,
And for us, bruis'd and torn!

Thy side with cruel spear transpiers'd,
Let out a saving flood,
To wash our sinful stains away,
Of water mix'd with blood.

O heavenly manna! be our food,
Whilst in this life we stay;
And when death comes, prepare our souls
To meet the judgment day.
O gracious Jesus! bounteous Lord!
O Mary's clement Son!
Let sinners grace and pardon find,
Before thy mercy's throne.

*The following Anthems to the Blessed Virgin
are sometimes added.*

Solo. Sub tuum praesidium confugimus, sancta Dei genitrix!
Chorus. Sub tuum, &c.
Solo. Nostras deprecationes ne despicias in necessitatibus nostris.
Chorus. Sub tuum, &c.
Solo. Sed a periculis cunctis libera nos semper, ergo gloriosa et benedicta!
Chorus. Sub tuum, &c.

The same in English.

O HOLY Mother of our God!
To thee for help we fly;

Despise not this our humble prayer,
But all our wants supply.

O glorious Virgin, ever bless'd!
Defend us from our foes;
From threat'ning dangers set us free,
And terminate our woes.

Solo. O SANCTISSIMA, O purissima,
Dulcis Virgo Maria!
Ch. Mater amata, intemerata!
Ora, ora pro nobis.
Solo. Tota pulchra es, O Maria!
Et macula non est in te.

Ch. Mater ameta, &c.
Solo. Sicut lilium inter spinas,
Sic Maria inter filias,
Ch. Mater amata, &c.

TANTUM ergo Sacramentum.
Veneretnur cernui
Et antiquum documentum
Novo cedat ritui.
Praestet fides supplementum
Sensuum defectui.

Genitori, Genitoque
Laus et jubilatio,
Salus honor, virtus quoque
Sit et benedictio;
Proceddnti ab utroque
Compar sit laudatio. Amen.

EXERCISE

OF

𝕿𝖍𝖊 𝖂𝖆𝖞 𝖔𝖋 𝖙𝖍𝖊 𝕮𝖗𝖔𝖘𝖘

NOTE. — The opening prayers are to be said before the Altar.

IN the name of the Father, and of the Son, and of the Holy Ghost. Amen.

Blessed be the Most Holy and undivided Trinity, now and for ever more. Amen.

V. Thou O Lord, wilt open my lips,

R. And my tongue shall announce thy praise.

V. Incline unto my aid, O God.

R. O Lord, make haste to help me.

V. Glory be to the Father, and to the Son, and to the Holy Ghost.

R. As it was in the beginning, is now, and ever shall be. Amen.

Let us pray.

Direct, we beseech Thee, O Lord, our actions by thy holy inspirations, and carry them on by thy gracious assistance, that every prayer and work of ours may commence always with Thee, and by Thee be happily ended: Through Christ Jesus our Lord. Amen.

A PRAYER TO DIRECT THE INTENTION

LORD Jesus Christ, Saviour of my soul, I present myself before Thee to follow the Way of thy Cross and to retrace in spirit that sacred path, which was watered with Thy adorable blood during Thy painful journey to Calvary's Mount: I offer to Thee this pious exercise with the view of gaining the indulgences, which the Sovereign Pontiffs have attached to it: and I propose to pray for all the intentions, which they had in view in dispensing so rich a treasure. Grant me, O Lord, the dispositions necessary for obtaining these indulgences, as well for myself; as for the souls in purgatory, and in particular for those, for whom I design to pray. May I by this holy exercise merit your mercy in this world, so as to secure, with those suffering souls, a place in your eternal kingdom in the life to come. Amen.

And thou, O Blessed Mother of God, assist me by thy powerful intercession. Present this my feeble homage to thy Divine Son, in reparation of the many injuries He daily receives from bad Christians and from so many impious men, "*who deny Him that bought them.*" Let me participate in that ineffable sorrow, which pierced thy most tender soul during the several stages of His passion: that I may reap an abundant fruit from this holy exercise, for the advantage and ultimate salvation of my own soul, and the benefit of all those for whom I pray. Amen.

While proceeding towards each Station, a stanza of the "Stabat Mater" *may be said or sung*:

1. STABAT Mater, dolorosa,
   Juxta crucem lacrymosa,
   Dum pendebat filius.

———

FIRST STATION

V. We adore thee, O Lord Jesus Christ, and bless thy holy name:

R. Because by thy holy Cross thou hast redeemed the world.

Jesus is condemned to death.

LET us consider the wonderful submission of Jesus, when he received this unjust sentence. Let us reflect; that it was not Pilate alone who condemned him, but that all here present, and all the sinners of the world cried aloud for his death. Let us, therefore, penetrated with the most lively sorrow, say to him:

O adorable Jesus! since it is our crimes that have sentenced you to death, grant that we may detest them with our whole heart, and that our sincere repentance may obtain for us mercy and pardon.

Our Father. Hail Mary. Glory be to the Father,

V. Have mercy on us, O Lord.

R. Have mercy on us.

V. May the souls of the faithful departed, through the mercy of God, rest in peace.

R. Amen.

2. Cujus animam gementern,
   Contristatam et dolentem,
   Pertransivit gladius.

———

SECOND STATION

V. We adore thee, O Lord Jesus Christ, and bless thy holy name:

R. Because by thy holy Cross thou hast redeemed the world.

Jesus takes the Cross on his shoulders.

LET us consider with what meekness our divine Master takes on his mangled and bloody shoulders, the terrible instrument of his punishment. He thus wished to teach us how to carry our cross, by accepting with the greatest resignation, the sufferings that shall be inflicted on us by our heavenly Father, and those which we may endure from our fellow creatures.

O meek Jesus! It was we, miserable sinners, who are guilty of all kinds of iniquity, that should have carried this cross, and not you; for you were innocent. Grant us then strength to imitate your example, by enduring, without a murmur, all the trials of this life, which, in the order of your fatherly Providence, may enable us to satisfy your justice, and to arrive at our heavenly country. Our Father. Hail Mary. Glory be to the Father.

V. Have mercy on us, O Lord.

R. Have mercy on us.

V. May the souls of the faithful departed, through the mercy of God, rest in peace.

R. Amen.

3. O quam tristis et afflicta,
   Fuit illy benedicta
   Mater unigeniti!

———

THIRD STATION

V. We adore thee, O Lord Jesus Christ, and bless thy holy name:

R. Because by thy holy Cross thou hast redeemed the world.

Jesus falls the first time under the Cross.

LET us consider Jesus Christ beginning his painful journey to Calvary. The blood which he lost when he was scourged and crowned with thorns, has weakened him to such a degree, that he falls under the heavy load. He rises again, after the most cruel outrages, which he endures without betraying the least emotion of resentment. Behold how he thus wished to atone for our many falls, and to teach us to rise again, by the austerities of penance, when we have had the misfortune to fall into the abyss of sin.

O Good Jesus! stretch forth your succoring hand, and assist us amidst all the dangers to which we are exposed. Vouchsafe to strengthen us in our weaknesses, that after having courageously followed you to Calvary, we may there taste the delicious fruits of the tree of life, and become eternally happy with you.

Our Father. Hail Mary. Glory be to the Father.

V. Have mercy on us, O Lord.

R. Have mercy on us.

V. May the souls of the faithful departed, through the mercy of God, rest in peace.

R. Amen.

4. Quae moerebat et dolebat,
   Pia mater, dum videbat
   Nati poenas inclyti.

FOURTH STATION

V. We adore thee, O Lord Jesus Christ, and bless thy holy name:

R. Because by thy holy Cross thou host redeemed the world.

Jesus meets his most afflicted Mother.

LET us consider how painful it was to this divine Son, to meet his most beloved Mother under such afflicting circumstances; and how heart rending it was to Mary to behold her adorable Son, dragged along by a troop of ruffians, through an immense crowd, who load him with reproaches. At this sight, her maternal heart is pierced with a thousand swords, and is torn with all anguish. She wished to deliver our Saviour, and to rescue him from the hands of his executioners; but she knows that the work of our salvation is to be thus accomplished. Uniting then the sacrifice of her love to that of her Son, she participates in all his sufferings, and accompanies him, even to his last breath.

O Mary! Mother of Sorrows! obtain for us that ardent love with which you accompanied Jesus to that holy mountain, and that constancy which you displayed at the foot of the cross, in order that we may faithfully remain there with you, and that nothing may be ever able to separate us from thence.

Our Father. Hail Mary. Glory be to the Father.

V. Have mercy on us, O Lord.

R. Have mercy on us.

V. May the souls of the faithful departed, through the mercy of God, rest in peace.

R. Amen.

5. Quis est homo qui non fleret,
   Christi matrem si videret
   In tanto supplicio?

———————

FIFTH STATION

V. We adore thee, O Lord Jesus Christ, and bless thy holy name:

R. Because by thy holy Cross thou hast redeemed the world.

Jesus is assisted in carrying his Cross by Simon of Cyrene

LET us consider the great goodness of Jesus Christ towards us. Though he allows himself to be assisted in carrying his cross, it is not because he wants strength, it being his powerful hands that sustain the world; but he was anxious to teach us to unite our sufferings to his, and to drink with him of his chalice of bitterness.

O Jesus, our Master! You have drank the most bitter portion of this chalice, and you have left the smallest to our share. Do not suffer us to be such enemies to ourselves, as to refuse it. Enable us, on the contrary, to accept it cheerfully, that we may become worthy of drinking in the torrent of delights with which you inebriate your elect in the land of the living.

Our Father. Hail Mary. Glory be to the Father.

V. Have mercy on us, O Lord.

R. Have mercy on us.

V. May the souls of the faithful departed, through the mercy of God, rest in peace.

R. Amen.

6. Quis posset non contristari
   Pian matrem contemplari
   Dolentem cum filio

———————

SIXTH STATION

V. We adore thee, O Lord Jesus Christ, and bless thy holy name:

R. Because by thy holy Cross thou hast redeemed the world.

Veronica wipes the face of Jesus

LET us consider the heroic action of this holy woman, who presses through the crowd of soldiers to behold her divine Master. She sees that he is covered all over with spittle, dust, perspiration, and blood. The painful sight afflicts her soul, even to tears; and her love, placing her above all fear, she approaches Jesus, and wipes his disfigured countenance; that august countenance) which ravishes all the Saints, and before the splendor of which, the Angels veil their faces with their wings.

O Jesus! the most beautiful among the sons of men! to what a condition has your love for us reduced you! Oh, never were you more worthy of our adorations and homage than now! We adore you, therefore; and prostrate before your divine Majesty, we beseech you to remember no more our many offences, and to restore to our soul its ancient beauty, which it has lost by sin.

Our Father. Hail Mary. Glory be to the Father.

V. Have mercy on us, O Lord.

R. Have mercy on us.

V. May the souls of the faithful departed, through the mercy of God, rest in peace.

R. Amen.

7. Pro peccatis suae gentis,

Vidit Jesum in tormentis,
Et flagellis subditum.

SEVENTH STATION

V. We adore thee, O Lord Jesus Christ, and bless thy holy name:

R. Because by thy holy Cross thou hast redeemed the world.

Jesus falls under the Cross the second time

LET us consider the Man–God falling again under his grievous Load. Let us behold this victim stretched along the ground, under the terrible wood of his sacrifice, exposed anew to the cruelty of his executioners, and the soldiers. It was in order to give us a further proof of his infinite love, that Jesus Christ permitted this second fall. He also wished to teach us, that as we so often relapse into sin, we should never lose our confidence in his mercy — that in the midst of the greatest afflictions, we should not be discouraged — that the road to heaven is filled with briars and thorns, and that in order to share in his glory, we must pass through the crucible of suffering.

Jesus, our strength! Preserve us from every relapse — save us from the misfortune of losing our immortal souls, and of thus rendering useless all the suffering and fatigue which you endured to deliver us from eternal death.

Our Father. Hail Mary. Glory be to the Father.

V. Have mercy on us, O Lord.

R. Have mercy on us.

V. May the souls of the faithful departed, through the mercy of God, rest in peace.

R. Amen.

8. Vidit suum dulcem natum,
   Morientem, desolatum.
   Dum emisit spiritum.

EIGHTH STATION

V. We adore thee, O Lord Jesus Christ, and bless thy holy name:

R. Because by thy holy Cross thou hast redeemed the world.

*Jesus consoles the women of Jerusalem, who
followed him, and wept over him.*

LET us here admire the noble generosity of our Divine Lord. He seems to forget his own sufferings altogether, to administer consolation to those holy women, who were plunged in the deepest grief at his deplorable state. He exhorts them, not to weep for him, but rather for themselves, and their ungrateful, perfidious country. He has thus taught us, that our compassion for his sufferings, will make little impression on his tender heart, unless we bewail our sins, which are the sole cause of all his agony.

O amiable Jesus, true comforter of afflicted Souls! vouchsafe to look down upon us with tenderness and mercy. Grant us grace to walk constantly after you, on the royal road of the cross, that like the women of Jerusalem we may hear the words of life, and enjoy your unspeakable consolations.

Our Father. Hail Mary. Glory be to the Father.

V. Have mercy on us, O Lord.

R. Have mercy on us.

V. May the souls of the faithful departed, through the mercy of God, rest in peace.

R. Amen.

9. Eia mater, fons amoris,
   Me sentire vim doloris
   Fac, ut tecum lugeam.

NINTH STATION

V. We adore thee, O Lord Jesus Christ, and bless thy holy name:

R. Because by thy holy Cross thou hast redeemed the world.

Jesus falls under the Cross the third time.

LET us consider our adorable Jesus arrived at the summit of Calvary. He directs his eyes to. the spot where he is soon to be sacrificed to the fury of his enemies. His attention is engaged at this moment by our endless relapses, and the great number of sinners, for whom his blood will be shed in vain. This cruel thought afflicts his tender heart, more than all the punishment which he has yet to endure. It fills his soul with a profound sorrow, and his strength failing him, as in his agony, he falls on his face to the earth.

O Jesus, Victim of Love! Behold you are at length going to be immolated for the salvation of mankind. Deign to apply to our soul's the merits of your sacrifice in this life, that we may offer you the sacrifice of our praises during all eternity.

Our Father. Hail Mary. Glory be to the Father.

V. Have mercy on us, O Lord.

R. Have mercy on us.

V. May the souls of the faithful departed, through the mercy of God, rest in peace.

R. Amen.

10. Fac ut ardcat cor meum,
    In amando Christum Deum,
    Ut illi complaceam.

TENTH STATION

V. We adore thee, O Lord Jesus Christ, and bless thy holy name:

R. Because by thy holy Cross thou hast redeemed the world.

Jesus is stripped of his garments.

LET us consider how much our dear Redeemer suffered, when his executioners stripped off his garments. All the wounds which he had received, and by which his clothes adhered to his sacred flesh, were now torn open, and thus the pain of his bloody scourging was renewed. But what he most sensibly felt was, to see himself exposed, in a state of nakedness, before such an immense multitude.

O Jesus, divine Lamb! you have at length come to the place of slaughter, without opening your mouth to complain. Ah, how forcible and how eloquent is your silence! With what efficacy it teaches us the necessity of repressing our impatience and our murmurs! You suffer yourself to be stripped of all your garments, to expiate our misfortune, in having lost the precious gift of grace. Oh, grant that we may recover that inestimable treasure, that we may entirely put off the old man, and be clothed with the new, according to you, so that we may henceforth live according to the sentiments of your adorable heart.

Our Father. Hail Mary. Glory be to the Father.

V. Have mercy on us, O Lord.

R. Have mercy on us.

V. May the souls of the faithful departed, through the mercy of God, rest in peace.

R. Amen.

11. Sancta mater, istud agas,
Crucifixi fige plagas
Cordi meo valide.

ELEVENTH STATION

V. We adore thee, O Lord Jesus Christ, and bless thy holy name:

R. Because by thy holy Cross thou hast redeemed the world.

Jesus is nailed to the Cross

LET us consider Jesus Christ offering himself to his executioners to be crucified, and stretching himself out on the wood of the cross. Oh! what torment does he not endure whilst the heavy strokes of the hammer are driving the nails into his feet, and his adorable hands! His flesh is torn, his bones are bruised, his nerves are broken, his veins are burst asunder! His blood flowing in great torrents, exhausts his strength, and adds to his other terrible sufferings, that of the most burning thirst.

O sin! accursed sin! It was you plunged into that ocean of sorrow the victim of our salvation. Ah! Christian, what an excess of love! what immense charity! Shall not our hearts be rent asunder with grief, and burn with love at this dreadful sight! will they not renounce all the pleasures of the world! Shall they not be ever crucified with that of Jesus, and will not our eyes pour forth torrents of tears both day and night!

Our Father. Hail Mary. Glory be to the Father.

V. Have mercy on us, O Lord.

R. Have mercy on us.

V. May the souls of the faithful departed, through the mercy of God, rest in peace.

R. Amen.

12. Tui Nati vuinerati,
   Tam dignati pro me pati.
   Poenas mecum divide.

TWELFTH STATION

V. We adore thee, O Lord Jesus Christ, and bless thy holy name:

R. Because by thy holy Cross thou hast redeemed the world.

Jesus expires on the Cross

LET us consider Jesus the God of all sanctity, expiring between two malefactors, and let us admire the sweetness and strength of his love. He prays to his Father for the pardon of his murderers. He promises heaven to the good thief. He recommends his Mother to his beloved disciple.. He commits his soul to the hands of his Father. He announces that all is consummated, and he expires for us. At the same moment all creatures proclaim his Divinity. All nature mourns, and seems anxious to annihilate itself, on beholding the death of its Creator.

O sinners! will you be the only exception to this general mourning? Will you alone remain insensible before this heart-rending spectacle? Cast one look upon your Saviour, and see the frightful state for which your sins have reduced him. Nevertheless, he forgives you, if your repentance be sincere. His feet are nailed to await your coming. His arms are stretched out to receive you. His side is opened, and his heart wounded to pour out all his graces upon you. His head is bowing down to give you the kiss of reconciliation and peace! Oh! let us all then run up to his cross, and let us die for him, as he has died for us!

Our Father. Hail Mary. Glory be to the Father.

V. Have mercy on us, O Lord.

R. Have mercy on us.

V. May the souls of the faithful departed, through the mercy of God, rest in peace.

R. Amen.

13. Fac me tecum pie flere,
   Crucifixo condolere,
   Donec ego vixero.

THIRTEENTH STATION

V. We adore thee, O Lord Jesus Christ, and bless thy holy name:

R. Because by thy holy Cross thou hast redeemed the world.

Jesus is taken down from the Cross

LET us consider the overwhelming grief of his tender Mother after the death of her Divine Son Jesus. She receives this precious deposit in her arms. She gazes on his pale, bloody, and disfigured countenance. She sees his eyes closed, his mouth shut, his side opened, and his hands and feet pierced through. This sight is to her an unspeakable martyrdom, the value of which God alone can comprehend.

O Mary! we, we alone are the cause of your affliction; and it is our sins that have pierced through your soul, by fastening Jesus to the cross. O Mother of Mercy! vouchsafe to obtain our pardon, and permit us to adore in your arms our crucified Love. Imprint so strongly in our souls, the sorrows which you feel at the foot of the cross, that we may never lose the recollection of them.

Our Father. Hail Mary. Glory be to the Father.

V. Have mercy on us, O Lord.

R. Have mercy on us.

V. May the souls of the faithful departed, through the mercy of God, rest in peace.

R. Amen.

14. Juxta crucem tecum stare,
Et tibi me sociare
In planctu desidero.

———————

FOURTEENTH STATION

V. We adore thee, O Lord Jesus Christ, and bless thy holy name:

R. Because by thy holy Cross thou hast redeemed the world.

Jesus is laid in the Sepulchre

BEHOLD then, O Jesus, our dear Redeemer! behold the spot where your adorable body, the precious pledge of our salvation is reposed. Grant, that our greatest comfort in this valley of tears may be to meditate on the sufferings and ignominous death which you endured for our deliverance. You wished to be placed in a new sepulchre, to give us to understand, that we must approach you in the sacrament of your love, with a new heart. Vouchsafe to purify us from all our stains, and to render us worthy to assist frequently at your holy banquet.

Bury in the same tomb all our iniquities, that we may die to our passions and to very thing earthly, to lead with you a life hidden in God, and thus deserve a happy end, and the blissful vision of you in the splendor of your glory.

Our Father. Hail Mary. Glory be to the Father.

V. Have mercy on us, O Lord.

R. Have mercy on us.

V. May the souls of the faithful departed, through the mercy of God, rest in peace.

R. Amen.

(On returning to the Altar, recite the following prayers:)

Antiphon. Christ became obedient for us unto death, even the death of the Cross.

V. By thy Holy Cross deliver us, O God.

R. From all our enemies.

Let us pray

Look down, we beseech Thee, O eternal Father, on this thy family, for which our Lord Jesus Christ was pleased to be delivered into the hands of the wicked and to suffer the torment of the cross who liveth and reigneth, one God in unity with Thee and the Holy Ghost, forever and ever. *R*. Amen.

Antiphon. O all ye, that pass by the way, attend and see if there be grief like unto my grief.

V. Pray for us, O most sorrowful Mother of God.

R. That we may be made worthy of the promises of Christ.

Let us pray

We beseech thee, O Lord Jesus Christ that the Blessed Virgin Mary, who during Thy bitter passion, had her most holy soul pierced, with the sword of sorrow, may effectually intercede for us with Thy clemency, both now and at the hour of death. Who livest and reignest, one God with the Father and the Holy Ghost, for ever and ever. *R*. Amen.

Antiphon. It is a holy and wholesome thought to pray for, the dead, that they may be loosed from their sins.

V. Eternal rest give unto them, O Lord.

R. And let perpetual light shine upon them.

Let us pray

O God, the Creator and Redeemer of all the faithful, grant to the souls of Thy servants departed the remission of all their sins, that through pious supplications they may obtain that pardon, which they have always desired. Who livest and reignest one God for ever and ever, *R*. Amen.

(Our Father, &c., Hail Mary, &c., Glory be to the Father, &c. Each to be recited six times.)

V. Jesus Christ crucified have mercy on us.

R. Have mercy on us, O Lord, have mercy on us.

V. And may the souls of the faithful departed, through the mercy of God, rest in peace.

R. Amen.

————————

Various Books Published By

CONFEDERATE STATES PRINTING OFFICE[6]

You can find these fine books and others by C.S. Publishing Office at your favorite Bookseller, or at www.lulu.com

The Confederate States of America in Prophecy, by Rev. W.H. Seat, a Southern Methodist Minister, and is edited by Dr. William G. Peters. This work examines Daniel's prophecy of the of the Five Governments; with the United States as the Fifth Government and the Confederate States as the little stone cut from the mountain, as a revived Government of Judah.

The Eschatology of the United States as Restored Israel, and the Confederate States as a Restored Judah, is a secular prophecy of the people of North America as God's special chosen people.

In the heady days of Southern victories over Northern armies, Rev. Seat posits the future history of the Confederate States based upon the Prophet Daniel.

Sermons of the Confederacy 1861-1862, edited by Dr. William G. Peters, is a collection of sermons by Southern ministers, bishops, and priests, from 1861-1862.

These ministers cover, in their sermons and discourses, a wide range of subjects, from the cause of the War, differences between Yankees and Southerners, Negroes and their purpose among Southerners, the life and death of Confederate heroes, service to God, military service and Christian Faith, etc.

This is an excellent book for those who want to understand our Confederate ancestors, the C.S.A., and the South's Faith in God and victory in the face of implacable Northern invasion.

Sermons of the Confederacy 1863-1865, edited by Dr. William G. Peters, is a collection of sermons by Southern ministers, bishops, priests, and rabbi from 1863-1865, and a continuation from "Sermons of the Confederacy 1861-1862."

These men of God cover a wide range of subjects, from the cause of the War, differences between Yankees and Southerners, Negroes and their purpose among Southerners, the life and death of Confederate heroes, service to God, military service and

---

[6] Also designated as C.S. Printing Office. A division of Confederate States of America, Inc.

Christian Faith, etc.

This is an excellent book for those who want to understand our Confederate ancestors, the C.S.A., and the South's Faith in God and victory in the face of death and destruction from Federal invasion.

The True Church Indicated to the Inquirer, by Bishop John McGill. Confederate Bishop of Richmond, Virginia, edited by Dr. William G. Peters.

Bp. McGill examines the claims of various and sundry groups to be the true Church. He examines these claims in the light of scripture, history, tradition and reason. Then he contrasts them against the claims of the Catholic Church to be the One, True Church, showing how the claims of all other groups fall short.

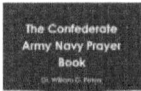

The Confederate Army Navy Prayer Book is the Episcopal Prayer Book for the Armed Services of the Confederacy, edited by Dr. William G. Peters. The Prayer Book went through annual editions from 1861-1865, and was the official military prayer book of the Confederate States.

Additional prayers have been included, including national calls to prayer by President Jefferson Davis throughout the War, and a sermon by Bp. Stephen Elliot delivered upon the Day of National Humiliation, Fasting and Prayer in 1861.

The Catholic Devotional for Confederate Soldiers was written by Bishop McGill for the Confederate soldiers to carry with them into battle, and for their encampments.

The work was published and registered by Bp. McGill in the Confederate States of America in 1861, and is edited by Dr. William G. Peters.

The Devotional contains many Catholic prayers, novenas, selections from the Mass, etc., which are appropriate to daily devotions, for Catholics and other Christians.

Faith The Victory by Bishop John McGill, Confederate Bishop of Richmond, Virginia, edited by Dr. William G. Peters.

Bp. McGill presents an explanation of Catholic doctrine for Catholics and non-Catholics who hold to the old orthodox Protestant beliefs and traditions, and want to know more about the development and meaning of Christian doctrine.

A non-polemical work, the Bishop provides a rational explanation of sometimes difficult subjects. It is a clear concise summary of doctrinal points of interest to all Christians, without being either too brief, or tedious.

www.ingramcontent.com/pod-product-compliance
Lightning Source LLC
LaVergne TN
LVHW011232080426
835509LV00005B/450